THE COUNTRY CHU

THE COUNTRY CHURCH

A Guide for the Renewal of Rural Christianity

ROBERT VAN DE WEYER

DARTON, LONGMAN AND TODD
LONDON

First published in 1991 by
Darton, Longman and Todd Ltd
89 Lillie Road, London SW6 1UD

© 1991 Robert Van de Weyer

ISBN 0–232–51946–3

A catalogue record for this book is available
from the British Library

Phototypeset in 10½/12pt Baskerville by Intype, London
Printed and bound in Great Britain by
Courier International Limited, East Kilbride

CONTENTS

Introduction   1

1. COMMUNITY   5
   What is a village?   5
   Who lives in my village?   11
   How does my village function?   17
   Who belongs to the church?   23
   What about the different denominations?   30

2. WORSHIP   38
   Is small beautiful?   38
   Is old beautiful?   44
   How can a handful sing hymns?   50
   How does one preach to a handful?   56
   Must it always be Communion?   63

3. MINISTRY   71
   What should the parson be up to?   71
   How can one parson cope with numerous
      villages?   78
   How can ministry be shared?   84
   Can lay people be pastors?   91
   How many clergy can we afford?   96

4. BUILDING   104
    Is the church the people or the building?   104
    How should we use our ancient pile?   110
    Can the church patronise local arts?   119
    Can we afford to maintain our church?   125
    When should a church be closed?   132

5. MISSION   139
    How can we proclaim the gospel in our village?   139
    How should we welcome newcomers?   145
    How should we respond to change in our village?   150
    Is God green?   156
    Yeast and light – and bells?   162

INTRODUCTION

During the course of the twentieth century a cloud of gloom has settled over the rural church. In many villages the population has declined, the habit of church-going has weakened, and so congregations have dwindled. The number of clergy has fallen steeply, so that one parson now covers four, five, six or even more villages. The cost of maintaining the church fabric has escalated, so that many congregations are condemned to a treadmill of jumble sales and coffee mornings merely to keep the water out. The consequence is that Christianity in the countryside seems to be caught in a vicious downward spiral. As the congregations get smaller, the buildings become damper and darker, the parsons become more harassed, and the services become progressively more depressing – so yet fewer people want to attend worship. There are then an even smaller number of people to raise funds to maintain the fabric, and clergy become more reluctant to serve in our villages.

The numerous books and reports published in recent decades about Christianity in the countryside have all struck an elegiac and plaintive note. They have lamented the long, slow disease infecting the country church, and have predicted its imminent demise. They have also deplored the neglect with which both the ecclesiastical authorities and the government treat rural life in general, and rural religion in particular. The scarcity of country parsons is linked to the disappearance of rural bus services, the closure of village schools and shops, and the poverty of many elderly village residents, to present a pitiful picture of decline and deprivation.

This book seeks to paint a rather different picture of rural life and faith. I am one of the growing number of refugees from the cities who in the past fifteen years have reversed the decline in rural population. I grew up in London, but in the mid-1970s moved with my family to Huntingdonshire, and for the past decade I have been an unpaid country parson, with four small villages. Congregations on a normal Sunday range from two to fifteen, so any attempt to imitate the busy, bustling style of worship of a modern suburban church is a ludicrous failure. Yet my parishioners have taught me a way of prayer, praise and preaching which, to my taste, is far more satisfying. And, recognising how little time I have to serve them, they have come to share the Christian ministry to an extent that even the most progressive city parish would envy. They have shown me too how to cherish the ancient buildings where we gather on Sunday, and have responded to my enthusiasm by taking on their own shoulders the perpetual fabric appeals. As a political economist by profession, I have come to see that our villages, not our cities, will be in the vanguard of social and political change in the coming decades, so the rural church has a vital prophetic role.

In short, it is high time that we allowed God's Spirit to blow away that cloud of gloom, and it is the purpose of this book to show how the Spirit can breathe new life and vision into the country church. There is nothing revolutionary in the ideas here, but they are radical in the proper sense of that term: we must go back to our roots, rediscovering those traditions which have given the rural church such serenity and resilience in past centuries. Nor do the proposals here require any special courage or insight from clergy or laity; on the contrary, this book is addressed to ordinary people in ordinary parishes. Above all, Christians in the countryside need confidence in their own spiritual instincts, and reassurance that, if they are true to those instincts, their church has a bright, secure future. I hope that country people reading this book will find themselves saying, time and again, 'Yes, that's exactly what I feel,' or 'Yes, that's exactly how I think things ought to be,' and, most of all, 'Yes, let's do that – it's just right for us.'

In 1990 the Church of England published *Faith in the Countryside*, a weighty report which was the product of a high-powered commission appointed by the Archbishop of Canterbury. It is filled with insights into the state of the rural church today, based on numerous interviews around the country, but, of course, it was never intended to be studied by ordinary people in the parishes. And, while it raised many questions, it is widely felt by those living in small villages that its recommendations are often impractical and unrealistic. This book is intended, in part at least, as a companion and complement to *Faith in the Countryside*. It is much shorter and, I hope, easy to read. It is also thoroughly practical – a kind of DIY manual for rural church life.

In addition to individuals reading it on their own, groups may find it valuable as a basis for discussion and reflection. It is divided into five chapters, each subdivided into five sections, so either the whole book, or a single chapter, could be studied during the five weeks (minus Holy Week) of Lent. The questions, which serve as titles to the five sections in each chapter, may also be used as springboards for discussion. You will find many quite definite and precise suggestions in these pages, but equally there are issues which are deliberately left open. Your church is special, with its own unique history and unique bunch of people that make up the congregation. So, as well as sharing the common renewal of the country church, you must rejoice in your own traditions and talents – and idiosyncrasies.

1

COMMUNITY

WHAT IS A VILLAGE?

We use the word 'village' to refer to a vast range of different
communities. At one extreme a hamlet of fifty or a hundred
people, with no shop, pub or school, may sometimes be
called a village. At the other, a settlement of five or even
ten thousand people, with housing estates around the edge
and a supermarket near the centre, may also be described
as a village. Oddly, other settlements of five or ten thousand
are called 'towns' or even, in exceptional cases, 'cities'. The
term 'village' also still attaches to some areas of large
conurbations, especially London, where, for example, the
people of Hampstead still 'go down to the village' to do
their shopping.

To qualify for the name 'village' in popular parlance, a
place must have two characteristics. Firstly, it should have
been a village in previous centuries, and have a centre
which retains some of the features of its rustic past. A
village green with a pond, plus a few timber-frame farm-
houses, is ideal; but a single street with a terrace of farm
cottages will do. Secondly, it must boast an ancient church.
A hamlet which has lost its church, or never had one, is
not usually called a 'village'; indeed, its own residents
usually do not think of it as such.

Equally, a settlement which has sprouted large housing

estates, and may even have overtaken the nearby market town in population, but which has a small, ancient church at its heart, may still be a 'village'. Conversely, Durham and Ely, which in living memory were no larger than many modern expanded villages, are deemed 'cities' because they are dominated by medieval cathedrals.

No harm comes from using the word 'village' so loosely – except when it applies to church policy. Bishops and pastoral committees, when surveying a map of their rural dioceses, seem often only dimly aware of the huge differences in church life and ministry between a place of fifty or a hundred inhabitants, and a settlement of a hundred times larger with five or ten thousand people. Both are referred to as 'villages', both are said to be 'rural', and so the spiritual and religious needs are taken to be much the same. The work-load of the rural clergy is popularly assumed to depend on the number of villages under his charge; yet a man with two villages may be ministering to twelve thousand people, while a man with seven or even ten villages may have less than a thousand souls in his care. As we shall see, numerous errors in ministry flow from this confusion.

To come to grips with the country church and to understand its particular spiritual challenges and problems today, we must begin by glancing backwards at the history of the village and thence come to some working definition.

The great majority of our villages were already settled a thousand years ago, and probably even before the Romans invaded two thousand years ago. Typically they were between two and five miles apart, so that a man could walk to the parish boundary in order to feed his livestock or collect wood, and then return home, within a couple of hours. The population was usually a few hundred. This was large enough for each village to have its own blacksmith, carpenter, wheelwright and other specialist craftsmen on whom agriculture depended. Yet it was small enough to be fed entirely by food grown within the parish, and to be housed and kept warm by wood chopped within the local copses. The village was thus economically and socially self-sufficient, even to the extent of people usually marrying from within the village. And, of course, everyone knew everybody else by name – and knew most of their business as well.

Since medieval times the village has undergone three quite distinct revolutions. The first was based on the change in land tenure, from communal to individual ownership. In the Anglo-Saxon village there were typically two large open fields, each of which could vary between five hundred and a thousand acres. One was used to grow hay for the livestock in winter, and the other was divided into narrow strips for cultivating grain and vegetables. Beyond the fields there was unfenced pasture for grazing, and woodland. Each family was allocated enough strips to feed itself, and enough hay for its animals; it was allowed to graze the animals on the common land in summer, and to collect a certain amount of wood each year. This system worked perfectly well so long as there was ample land, and the village was economically isolated.

In the two centuries after the Norman conquest the population almost tripled, so by the late thirteenth century pressure on land in some parts of England was intense. Moreover, both the church and the aristocracy had realised that fortunes could be made by rearing sheep and selling the wool to the weavers of Flanders. In village after village the church and the lord of the manor conspired to push the peasants off the open fields, and to divide the parish with hedges into small fields in which sheep could graze and crops be grown for sale in the expanding towns and cities. The bulk of the land went to the lord, a large slice was taken by the church, and the rest divided between a handful of families who were regarded with favour. The rest of the population had to work for wages for these new landowners.

This movement to 'enclose' the countryside took place gradually over five hundred years, reaching a climax in the seventeenth and eighteenth centuries, so that by 1800 virtually the whole of Britain was in private hands. The foundations were now laid for the second rural revolution.

In the early decades of the nineteenth century vast new factories were springing up in northern England, initially manufacturing cotton and woollen cloth, but then widening their range to produce almost every good which human beings require, apart from food itself. This industrial revolution in the cities undermined most of the traditional rural crafts, from spinning and weaving to the making of cutlery and crockery. The unemployed, impoverished labourers had no choice but to leave their village and seek work in a factory. By the end of the nineteenth century industrial methods were spreading to agriculture itself, with steam-powered ploughs and threshing-machines replacing both horse and man. So the number of workers required on the land began to fall dramatically. According to the 1801 census, about half the population was employed in farming; by 1901 it was less than a quarter. Sixty years later, thanks to the tractor and combine harvester, fewer than two per cent were required.

The most elderly inhabitants of today's villages witnessed the dire effects of this second revolution. In their childhood prior to the First World War, the village was still a flourishing community, its school brimming with children, and its street bustling with men and women going about their business. It could certainly field a football and cricket team, and probably one or two reserve teams as well. When they reached middle-age, however, their own children were leaving the village to seek work in local towns, pubs and shops were closing for lack of trade, the school was threatened with closure for lack of pupils, and the street was empty. As for sports, there were barely enough able-bodied men, let alone young enthusiasts, to fill the team sweaters. Within half a lifetime the typical village lost between half and three-quarters of its population, and the majority of those remaining were over fifty.

Our elderly villager has, however, witnessed during the last quarter of a century a third revolution, as fundamental as the first two. Some time in the late 1960s the tide of population began to turn. Those moving from village to town were, for the first time in history, outnumbered by those selling their urban homes and buying a house in a village. Though an accurate picture is hard to deduce from census figures, as many as three million people may by now have chosen the quiet of the countryside in favour of the noisy city. Furthermore, as the relatively high price of rural houses indicates, this number would be very much greater if there were no restrictions on new building.

Indeed, the shape of this shift has been largely determined by the planning authorities. In most counties the planners have divided villages into three categories. Firstly there are the 'major centres', where the population has been allowed to grow twenty, fifty or even a hundred times. A large secondary school has usually been built, a number of new housing estates have sprung up, and a range of shops and even a supermarket have been established. Secondly there are the 'minor centres', where building has been permitted mainly within the confines of the old village – 'infilling', to use the planners' jargon. This has allowed the population to increase, but not to its pre-industrial level, since modern houses occupy two or three times as much space as labourers' cottages. Some of the 'minor centres' can support a primary school and shop, but these can only survive by being used by other villages nearby.

Thirdly there are 'hamlets', where virtually no new building is allowed.

These distinctions are usually quite arbitrary, in that historically all three types of village were much the same size. Not surprisingly, many have doubted the wisdom of this type of rural planning, a point we shall explore in more depth in Chapter 5. But, when it comes to defining the 'village' in present circumstances, the planners' categories are vital.

In the distant past villages were large enough to be economically self-sufficient, and small enough for everybody to know one another by name. Self-sufficiency has long since been lost but socially, until the 1960s, almost all the ancient villages were still communities, in which a person could not have flu without all the neighbours knowing. This remains the case in the 'hamlets' and 'minor centres'. However, as most of their inhabitants would agree, the 'major centres' are socially akin to a suburb, but which happens to have green fields on all sides. Understandably, they cling to the term 'village', as the residents of Hampstead in London do, because the British imagination remains rooted in the countryside. Yet as far as their various social institutions are concerned, including the church, they function like their counterparts in suburbs and market towns.

Our rural population reached a peak in Roman times, then again in the early fourteenth century before the Black Death, and finally in the seventeenth and eighteenth centuries prior to industrialisation. In all three periods the largest villages reached fifteen hundred or even two thousand souls, with the majority somewhat under a thousand in population, and a few with less than two hundred. For our present purposes let this be the range of communities which we define as 'village'.

WHO LIVES IN MY VILLAGE?

People who have been born and bred in the countryside often claim to 'take people as I find them', and it is a justifiable boast. If newcomers to a village are polite, kind and generous, then in due course the old villagers will take them to their hearts, regardless of their accent, wealth, status or even race. Equally, if a newcomer is pushy, ambitious or stingy, then the old villagers will be cold and unwelcoming. Indeed, it is a chastening experience for many newcomers, accustomed to the anonymity of the city, to find themselves facing such close moral scrutiny.

Yet none of us can be divorced from our upbringing and the myriad other influences that have shaped our outlook. People who have spent the first forty years of their lives in London or Manchester will have different attitudes and expectations of village life, compared with people who grew up in the village. And among the old villagers themselves the farmer is a chip off a quite different block from the labourer who drives his tractor.

Until as recently as the 1950s one could analyse village society almost entirely in terms of 'class'. Between a quarter and a third of villages had someone within the parish who could be described as 'the squire'. He and his family were undoubtedly at the top of the social hierarchy. In some cases he owned all the farmland, as well as many of the houses within the village. In other cases he simply had the lion's share of the land. He usually farmed some of the land himself, employing his own staff, and rented the rest to others in the village. He rarely lived within the village, but had a large manor house with its own extensive gardens set apart from it. He and his wife set the tone of village society. Thus, for example, if she was keen on the Mother's Union or the Women's Institute, then branches would flourish within the village. If he enjoyed shooting, then the men of the village could look forward to many happy and lucrative days as beaters.

Just below the squire came the parson. The squire was often the patron of the living and, in earlier times, frequently appointed a relative, such as a nephew, or the son of a friend – Trollope's novels give a delightful picture of this process. On the same level as the parson came any other professional people in the village, such as the doctor. If the village lacked a resident squire, either because the main landowner lived elsewhere or because there was no dominant landowner, the parson and the doctor were at the top of the social ladder.

On the next rung down the ladder came the 'yeomen' farmers. These were families who either owned or rented small farms. They generally lived within the village in substantial houses, many of which are still standing. Depending on the size of the parish, a village might have between five and twenty such families, and these formed the backbone of village life, supporting the church and all the social institutions and events. Unlike the parson and the doctor, they never dined with the squire, but showed unshakeable loyalty and respect.

Then came the various craftsmen and tradesmen: the blacksmith, the farrier, the saddler, the carpenter (who was also the undertaker), the wheelwright, the baker, the butcher, the publican, the thatcher and so on. The social attitudes within this group varied widely. Some identified with the yeomanry, seeing themselves as solid pillars of the established order. Others, however, rejoiced in their own economic independence, feeling free to opt out of those aspects of village life of which they disapproved or they disliked. Not surprisingly, from the seventeenth century onwards, this class was the breeding-ground for the Nonconformist churches.

At the bottom came the labourers, who formed the

majority of the population. The men depended for work on the squire and the yeoman farmers and, while some were employed throughout the year, many were taken on only at haymaking and harvest. Almost all unmarried girls worked as servants for the squire, the parson and the yeomen farmers. They eked out their miserable livelihood with poultry, a pig and vegetables in their own gardens.

This old class system, although tottering, was still recognisable in the inter-war years, but since the Second World War it has been undermined by three main factors. Firstly, mechanisation, plus agricultural chemicals, has virtually eliminated the farm labourer, leaving less than 150,000 scattered across the country. The same process has also drastically reduced the number of yeoman farmers, since modern methods require far larger farms. As recently as twenty years ago there were half a million independent farms; today there is barely a third of that number. Secondly, almost all the old crafts and trades are now redundant, with the exception of that of the publican. The few craftsmen that survive, such as thatchers and blacksmiths, no longer serve the ordinary people of the village, but must look far afield for work, mainly from affluent newcomers to rural life. Thirdly, the old-fashioned squire is almost extinct, destroyed in part by heavy inheritance taxes, and in part by a change in social attitudes which revolts against his self-confident paternalism.

The modern village is, in one respect, classless. There is no social hierarchy, in which each group knows its place, and no one enjoys respect merely because of the station they hold in life. Yet the ancient classes have been replaced by four distinct social groups, each with its own attitudes and interests. They may be called the labourers, the professionals, the farmers and the retired.

The labourers are mostly to be found in council houses, built on the edge of the village soon after the Second World

War, but some live in old farm cottages. They are mostly tenants, but in recent years many have purchased their homes. In a typical village around a dozen labourers work on the land – less in eastern England where arable farming predominates, more in the north and west where livestock is reared. In addition, a number are employed outside the village as lorry-drivers, factory workers and the like. Most of the labourers were born and bred in the village, but as council houses and cottages have fallen vacant a surprising number of manual workers from local towns and cities have eagerly taken up residence in the countryside.

We should include in this first group the elderly who have spent all their lives in the village. Most are now widows whose husbands worked on the land. They hold within their memories the history of two of the rural revolutions described earlier, but sadly within the next two decades those memories will die with them.

The professionals are almost all newcomers to the village. Unlike the farmers and most of the labourers, whose livelihood ties them to the countryside, the professionals have chosen the village solely because it is a pleasant place in which to live. Until recently almost all the professionals worked outside the village, often travelling long distances to their offices, and paying thousands of pounds each year on fuel and rail tickets. Country living is thus, for most professionals, an expensive luxury. But in the past decade a new type of professional has moved into the village: his office is a room within the home, festooned with computers and fax machines by which he is wired both to colleagues and to customers. The number of people able to work in this way is likely to increase in the coming years, so the demand for electronic cottages in pretty villages will rise sharply.

In many professional families both husband and wife go out to work. During the years of child-rearing, however, most mothers stay at home, and these young professional mothers form a sub-group of their own. They often spend a lot of time in each other's company, forming close friendships, and they can be a dominant influence in many village institutions, including the church.

The farmers in most villages are numerically the smallest of the four groups. In a village in eastern England, where the farming is entirely arable, there may be only three or four farmers, each with a thousand or more acres. Even in northern and western Britain, where holdings are smaller, it is now unusual to find more than a dozen. Almost three-quarters of farmland today is owned by the farmers themselves, so most are comparatively affluent. None the less, agriculture remains an insecure business, with both the size of the harvest and the price obtained for it fluctuating widely, so that farmers rarely feel as rich as people who have their money in stocks and shares. Moreover, the farmer's wealth cannot be realised without destroying the farm itself; so although on paper the farmers are worth more than the professionals in the village, they generally have a lower standard of living and enjoy cheaper holidays and fewer luxuries.

Farming remains one of the few occupations (perhaps the only one) which passes from father to son. Although some farmers' sons choose to pursue other careers, a remarkable number go away for three years to agricultural college, and then return home. There are thus often three, or even four, generations living in the village and, like the young professional wives, such a farming dynasty can exert considerable power in village affairs.

The retired in many respects are akin to the professionals. Most British people, even if they have lived for sixty years in a noisy, bustling city, dream of moving to a cottage in the country, with roses climbing around the front door. The majority get no further than trying to turn their suburban house and garden into such an idyll. But in the past two or three decades growing numbers have realised their vision. They are thus, like the professionals, volunteers for village life. And they too must incur extra costs: a country cottage is likely to be more expensive than the same-sized house in town, and they must drive far greater distances to see friends and relatives and to do the shopping. They have, in many cases, pursued highly-paid professional jobs prior to retirement.

Two other small groups in the modern village should be mentioned. In those parts of the country popular for holidays, such as the West Country and parts of Wales, large numbers of cottages have been bought as second homes. Such temporary residents are regarded with profound ambivalence by the locals. While the local shop and pub may appreciate the trade they bring, a large number of cold, empty houses through the long winter months can seem to destroy the heart of the village. It is a credit to the kindness and tolerance of country people that the temporary residents receive such a warm welcome when they reappear at Easter.

The same areas that attract holiday-makers also prove magnets to craftsmen, who are colourful refugees from the urban jungle. Devon, Cornwall, Yorkshire, Pembrokeshire and Norfolk abound with potters, glass-blowers, hand-loom weavers and cabinet-makers. They too enjoy the beauty of these counties but, since tourists are their main customers, economic forces pull them there as well.

We shall look later in detail at the role of the clergyman in the modern village, but it is worth asking now where he fits among these various social groups. In the nineteenth and the early years of the present century, most country parsons grew up in the countryside. Today, however, they are generally drawn from suburbia, brought up in middle-class professional homes, so in attitude and spirit they are usually akin to the professional newcomers. That simple fact, as we shall see, explains many of the innocent misjudgements that modern country clergy make.

HOW DOES MY VILLAGE FUNCTION?

In a village in Herefordshire not long ago, a strip show was organised in the village hall to which only males were invited. To the vicar's surprise and horror no one raised any objection, and the show went ahead without causing even a ripple on the calm waters of local life. A couple of months later four people on the village hall committee proposed a major refurbishment of the hall, redecorating the walls and providing new furniture, and the group offered to organise the necessary fund-raising themselves. The vicar heard about this proposal in advance, and assumed that it would be warmly welcomed, especially as everyone agreed that the village hall was in a fairly tatty state. But to his surprise a tidal wave broke within the committee, which in a few days had swept across the village. Six members of the committee, including the chairman, wrote a public letter, which was circulated to every house, accusing the proposers of conspiracy. The four proposers wrote a public reply, in which they accused their opponents of irresponsibility in allowing the village hall to deteriorate. Soon the village was divided, with the different factions barely speaking to each other in the street.

This is an extreme example of a phenomenon which is familiar to most modern villages. To a detached observer, like the vicar, it seems to betray a quite absurd distortion of priorities. Yet on closer inspection the issue at stake was not the morality of striptease, nor the tattiness of the village hall, but the rivalry between different groups within the village. Although most people expressed mild disapproval

when asked by the vicar about the strip show, no one felt
threatened – the organisers were merely hiring the village
hall. But the proposal to refurbish the hall brought to the
surface a profound clash of outlook. The old residents –
the 'labourers' – had built the village hall forty years ago,
and had been content with quite a humble standard of
décor. The newcomers – the 'professionals' – wanted some-
where bright and smart in which to hold parties and social
functions. On the village hall committee the labourers,
through their own initial apathy, had ceded places to the
professionals, but now, as they saw control slipping from
their hands, they were fighting a final battle. Appeals by
the vicar for reason and common sense to prevail fell on
deaf ears: to the labourers their social survival within the
village was at stake.

The labourers and the professionals have in general two
quite different attitudes to the village, and the contrast
permeates almost every aspect of village life. The labourers,
especially those who grew up in the village, identify with
it. They define themselves not in terms of their work, but
according to their residence within the village. Indeed,
in most cases they will only seek employment which is
compatible with remaining in the village, and would prefer
to be unemployed than to move. Some involve themselves
in village and church activities, but they do not see such
involvement as necessary to earn their place as members
of the village community. They are villagers by right, and
will remain members of the community even if, as many
do, they opt out of village affairs entirely.

The professionals, on the other hand, participate eagerly
in village life, and often take a zealous pride in the appearance and well-being of the village. They enthusiastically
raise funds to improve village facilities (including the village hall) and they may work late into the evening trimming
hedges and mowing verges to win the local prize as 'best-

kept village'. Their personal identity lies not with the village, however, but with their careers, and if promotion is offered on the other side of the country then the very next day an estate agent's sign will appear. Indeed, some say quite openly that they regard seven or ten years as quite long enough to stay in one place, and look forward to a change.

There is a similar clash in moral and cultural values, although here the division is sometimes blurred. Many labourers possess shotguns to shoot rabbits and pigeons – and perhaps still to poach a few pheasants – and even those who do not shoot generally regard blood sports as quite natural. Many professionals, however, are quite shocked at this apparent callousness, and many express their disapproval in the most vehement tones. Another common area of dispute is over lights and pavements. To the professional, brought up in a city, it seems unarguable that street lights and solid pavements along the village streets are desirable. But to the labourer dark nights and muddy verges hold no worries – and he objects to paying high taxes to the parish council for such fripperies.

These direct disagreements may be fuelled by indirect economic resentments. The professionals in general have far higher incomes than the labourers. Luckily, this rarely causes actual envy, perhaps because village life has always been marked by large inequalities of wealth. But many labourers dislike the large 'executive-style' homes, with double or even triple garages, which are built for the affluent professionals. More poignantly, the labourers, especially the older ones, hold the newcomers largely responsible for the decline in public transport to the village. Within living memory almost everyone, including sometimes the squire, depended on the bus to take them into town; so the bus company could put on a regular service. Today the new professionals never need public transport,

so bus services have either been totally withdrawn or are
so infrequent as to be virtually useless. Thus the elderly
residents without a car find themselves stranded. The professionals may respond, with impeccable justice, that the
bus would still have disappeared even if they had never
come to the village; yet it is their affluence, compared with
the poverty of earlier generations, which has wrought the
damage.

Inevitably these clashes and resentments find expression
in village politics. In many villages the professionals have
started their own groups and societies to which they almost
exclusively belong. These can include an amenity or conservation society, and a social or recreation committee to put
on dances, '60s' evenings and the like. In themselves these
pose no threat to other groups in the village, and may
even be welcomed as 'bringing new life' to the community.
Problems arise when the professionals quite properly want
to be represented on the basic village bodies, such as the
parish council and the village hall committee. In each
village the points of dispute will vary, but the underlying
anxieties and tensions will be the same.

Yet it would be quite wrong to see the modern village
as hopelessly divided. On the contrary, many villages have
learned to handle this 'third revolution' with great skill and
goodwill. The different groups have come to respect and
even to like one another, and as the years pass their values
and attitudes begin to fuse. For those villages where conflict
remains bitter and tensions high, it is instructive to see the
ways in which the gulf can be crossed. Typically there are
five (or perhaps six) groups which may act as bridges.

The first group is the farmers. As we have seen, their
numbers today are quite small. But, if they choose, they
can exercise disproportionate influence. Their strength is
that in attitudes and values they often hover between the
professionals and the labourers. Like the labourers they

identify with the village, having lived there since childhood. But they may have been sent away to boarding school, and probably also attended college, acquiring in the process a broader perspective. Moreover, their comparative affluence enables them to share the same interests and amusements as the professionals – farmers can be found on the Swiss ski slopes and the Greek beaches, along with bankers and lawyers. The farmers, if they bother to sit on the parish council and the village hall committee, can often enjoy everyone's trust, and find a middle course acceptable to all. And if they patronise social functions, it is more likely that all groups within the village will come – and getting a little tiddly together can do wonders for social harmony.

The second group is the retired. They, like the professionals, came from outside, and carry with them the values of suburbia. They too will often show great enthusiasm for 'improving' the village, but age confers on most of us a mellow tolerance of the views of others. Moreover, a retired person who does not go out to work, and hopes to be buried in the churchyard, has both the time and the interest to make friends with everyone. As a result most retired newcomers, by the age of seventy-five or eighty, have come to identify with the village almost as closely as those who were born there.

The third group are the young mums. Childbirth and motherhood, like death, are great levellers. The challenges and anxieties of bringing up a toddler are the same in a council house as in an 'executive' home. In addition a village, unlike a town or city, can have only one mother-and-toddler group and one playgroup, to which all mothers come. Moreover, apart from the small minority sent away for education, all the children attend the village school, so all the mothers meet at the gate at three o'clock. Difference of background and income are soon forgotten as natural human friendships are forged.

The fourth group are the cricket and football enthusiasts. Sport too is a great leveller. If someone has the energy to start a cricket or football club, players will appear from all groups in the village. Cricket in particular is a game which has flourished in rural England since the eighteenth century, with squire and servant standing shoulder to shoulder in the field. Although it is declining in our schools, it is enjoying an astonishing revival in our villages, with professional and labourer side by side.

The fifth group, somewhat oddly, is the cleaning ladies. In past centuries the relationship between servant and master was often extremely close, softening the potential animosity between the classes. Today the new professional families, especially those where both husband and wife have jobs, also require servants, in the form of cleaning ladies and nannies. Nannies are usually recruited from outside the village, but cleaning ladies must of necessity be found locally, and it is, of course, the labourer's families which provide them. Happily it is a seller's market, so wages now are quite reasonable, causing a small but significant transfer of wealth within the village. Cleaning ladies also frequently get to know their employers quite intimately and come to regard them as friends.

The sixth group is, happily, the church. There are unfortunately too many cases where the church is in effect hijacked by one group within the village – usually, but not always, the professionals – so alienating the rest. Without realising what he or she is doing, the minister colludes in this process. Yet if this trap can be avoided, the church can be the most powerful and effective force for unity within the village – and that, after all, is what Jesus came to preach.

WHO BELONGS TO THE CHURCH?

In 1597 Richard Hooker, one of the founding fathers of the Church of England, wrote: 'With us one society is both Church and Commonwealth . . . which people are not part of them the Commonwealth, and part of them the Church of God, but the selfsame people whole and entire.' In Hooker's mind the church and the nation were coterminous, every citizen of England belonging to the church. Yet even as Hooker wrote those famous words, there were growing numbers of clergy and laity who believed that such an attitude undermined the Christian faith. To them a person should only belong to the church if he has made a personal commitment to Jesus Christ as his Lord and Saviour. To embrace the adulterous wife and drunken vagrant within the church was, in their view, to make a mockery of the Gospel.

In the villages of England this theological dispute rumbles on. However, it is no longer conducted between different factions within the church, but takes place in the minds of individuals. Vicars and laity alike hover uneasily between both views, sometimes coming down on Hooker's side, and sometimes striving to emphasise personal commitment. Thus, for example, a vicar might encourage the entire village to attend harvest thanksgiving, and be delighted at the huge numbers turning out for the Christmas carol service. But when those occasional church-goers ask for their children to be baptised, he shows marked reluctance, perhaps insisting that they first undergo some course of instruction on Christian upbringing. The vicar may argue that carol services and harvest festivals are a form of evangelism, while baptism signifies firm faith, yet such fine distinctions tend to be lost on his parishioners, and he is regarded as awkwardly inconsistent.

Nevertheless, far from blaming vicars for their confusion,

we must recognise that there are profound spiritual issues
at stake, which are not easy to resolve. In the early church
Christianity was undoubtedly a matter of personal commitment. Individuals made a deliberate decision to follow
Jesus, often suffering terrible persecution as a consequence.
There was no room for luke-warm, occasional Christianity;
it was all or nothing. Acts of worship were thus a gathering
of people who had made this leap of faith. The courage of
these first Christians, and the unshakeable bonds of love
forged between them by their common devotion to Jesus,
made Christianity astonishingly attractive; within less than
three centuries it had been adopted as the official religion
of the Roman Empire.

But this very success turned the original notion of Christian community on its head. Once the state itself upheld
Christianity, then the whole population officially belonged
to the church. In the towns and villages of Europe the
bishops and priests were no longer striving to convert
people, but rather to ensure they put into practice a faith
they already (in theory) professed. Christianity changed
from a missionary faith to a pastoral religion, and that was
how it remained for over a millennium. Europe in the
Middle Ages could without question be described as a
'Christian culture', in which Christian beliefs permeated
every aspect of life, from politics to agriculture, from sex
to architecture.

By the sixteenth century, however, the pendulum was
already swinging back. Responding to a revival of secular
attitudes, the Protestant reformers sought to re-emphasise
personal faith. Although Luther and Calvin themselves still
tried to maintain the Christian state, later Protestants saw
clearly that a church based on individual commitment
could never embrace a whole nation, so that the links
between church and state must be severed. The Church of
England, however, found itself caught in a dilemma – in

which, in rural areas at least, it still remains. Its original leaders, such as Cranmer, Ridley and Latimer, were undoubtedly profoundly influenced by Protestant teaching, yet they, and the English people generally, still clung tenaciously to the ideal of a Christian nation, in which the doctrines and rituals of the church guided the affairs of town and village, merchant and politician.

The bitter ecclesiastical conflicts of the seventeenth and eighteenth centuries centred on this dilemma. The Puritans, followed more strongly by the Evangelicals, wanted the church to be a gathering of God's faithful people, drawn together by a burning love of Christ and sharing a common conviction of their own salvation. Although they acknowledged that God alone can make this distinction with certainty, they drew a clear line between those who were Christian, and therefore assured of eternal blessing, and those who had rejected the Gospel. While this wing of English Christianity attracted numerous adherents from every class of society, the majority recoiled from its apparently harsh implications. High churchmen, like Archbishop Laud, sought to reassert the pre-eminent position held by the church in medieval times, restoring in the process many Catholic rituals and festivals, while country parsons, like George Herbert, saw themselves as shepherds of everyone in the village, regardless of the quality of their faith.

The Puritans and Evangelicals lost most of the official battles but, as regards the towns and cities, largely won the war. When those hungry men and women left their ancestral villages in the nineteenth century to seek work in the new industrial cities, they abandoned their ancestral religion as well. Only a tiny minority of the Victorian working-classes attended worship, despite the efforts of rich benefactors to build huge, barn-like churches for them amid the grimy factories. Although the suburban middle classes were eager church-goers in the nineteenth century, by the middle years of the twentieth century they had followed the working-class example. In most urban and suburban areas only one or two per cent go to church on Sunday.

The consequence is that clergy and laity alike in our towns and cities have quite deliberately readopted the attitude of the first Christians: the church is a gathering of the faithful few. In some places they still maintain a few vestiges of civic religion – on Remembrance Sunday the vicar may lead a public ceremony which local dignitaries attend – and certain more picturesque urban churches remain popular for funerals and weddings, far beyond the circle of regular worshippers. Moreover, most Anglicans would be reluctant to follow the Puritans in condemning the unfaithful, and members of other religions, to everlasting perdition. But they clearly recognise that the majority is indifferent, or even hostile, to the Gospel; and in services and house-groups they strive with deep seriousness to discern how best to bear witness to Christ in a secular world.

The legal and liturgical changes in the Church of England in recent decades have strongly reinforced this outlook. Synodical government, from Parochial Church Councils up to the General Synod, requires parish churches to draw up an electoral roll. This in effect defines who is a member of the church – and by implication who is not a member. To Hooker and even Cranmer such a procedure would have been utterly repugnant, since in their view everyone by virtue of being English belongs to the Church of England. More subtly, the modern services also encourage a demarcation between member and non-member. Quite apart from the theology of the new services, which we will explore later, the old Book of Common Prayer was felt to belong to the whole community, its resonant phrases imbibed with mother's milk, while the 'alternative' services are the property solely of the faithful.

In the villages, however, the picture is starkly different.

Some are inclined to say that the countryside is fifty or a hundred years behind the times, and with education and encouragement should be made to catch up with the enlightened suburbs. Yet such a crude dismissal of the quirks of rural Christianity ignores the particular nature of village life, which gives Hooker's dictum continuing force. In a community where everyone knows everybody personally, people are naturally reluctant to draw lines of spiritual division. Indeed, the unavoidable social divisions described earlier create sufficient tension, without adding religious discord; and since typically the church includes worshippers from all social groups, people look to the church as a focus of unity.

This communal view of Christianity is expressed in the language people use about religion, and in their expectations of the church. People in villages talk freely of 'our church' and 'our vicar', phrases which today are quite foreign in towns and cities, where the great majority of inhabitants do not know the name of the vicar or minister in charge, and probably do not even know which is their parish church. Village people expect to be christened and married in the church, and buried in the churchyard, regardless of whether they attend worship regularly, and they regard it as a matter of the utmost importance that the major festivals are celebrated properly. Even the 'professionals', who were usually brought up in the city, quickly adopt these attitudes as part and parcel of the rural life which they have chosen.

To conclude, however, that Hooker's vision remains unchallenged and untainted in rural Britain would be to miss strong contrary forces, while any country parson that tries to imitate the ministry of George Herbert soon meets implacable opposition. The brute fact is that in the modern village, as in the city, most people do not seriously subscribe to the Christian creed, and still less do they acknowledge the Church's authority in moral and spiritual affairs. The vicar may be liked, and even respected, but he is not regarded as a font of any special wisdom or professional expertise – his long theological training often seems to count for nothing in people's eyes. Whereas in the past the leading members of the community were appointed churchwardens, exercising considerable power, today many country churches have difficulty in finding people to take the job. In the politics and social life of the village, the church and its officers are regarded as marginal, with neither a role to play nor any special influence to exert.

The clergy and the committed laity thus find themselves in a peculiar trap. On the one hand they want to uphold the unity and integrity of the village, and to this end they gladly put on harvest festivals, carol services, Mothering Sunday services and Remembrance services, to which the whole community can come. An anthropologist might observe that these services are like tribal rituals in which the village celebrates and reinforces its communal bonds – or, to use the modern jargon beloved by clergy, the services are expressions of 'folk religion'. On the other hand they wish, to some degree at least, to be evangelists and prophets, proclaiming the Gospel of Christ within the village, and urging people to embrace Christ as their Saviour. This, of necessity, requires them to admit openly that most people in the village are not Christians – and thus not full members of the church.

Fortunately, there is a way to square this circle, which at first sight seems false, but which is firmly rooted in Scripture. It consists in regarding the church as having two grades of member: the Old Testament members, and the New Testament members. Hebrew society described in the Old Testament conformed perfectly to Hooker's ideal. Everyone participated in the religious festivals and rituals, simply by virtue of being Hebrew, and their religious activities expressed and upheld the common values of the Hebrew people. Religion and society were unified. The church described in the New Testament, by contrast, was far closer to the Evangelical idea of Christian community. To become a member involved a profound act of faith, in which the individual decided to accept Jesus Christ as Lord. The two views of religion, however, are not opposed. Jesus was himself a devout Jew, and taught that his Gospel was the fulfilment of the Hebrew religion. Thus Peter, James, John and the other disciples were not required to renounce their old beliefs and practices, but to discover their full meaning through faith in Jesus.

Most people in a village have an Old Testament attitude to religion. They identify with the parish church simply by virtue of living in the village, and they want to participate in the harvest festival, the carol service and the rest to express their commitment to the community. Those major festivals in the rural calendar are no less acts of social solidarity than were similar festivals in the Hebrew calendar. Thus, just as Jesus upheld the old Hebrew religion, so we today ought to uphold the old rural religion – our 'folk religion'.

The handful of people who come to church Sunday by Sunday, and form the core of the Christian community, should be like Peter, James and John. They need not, and should not, reject or treat with contempt the folk religion of the village. On the contrary, they should rejoice in it, as a focus of evangelism. Just as the Passover festival of the Jews pointed towards Jesus, so too does our village harvest festival. The spiritual yearnings which draw people to these popular festivals have their fulfilment in the Gospel; and God, in his own good time, will reveal that to those whose hearts are open.

In short, therefore, everyone in the village belongs to the church, if they wish to regard themselves as members.

Vicars and the committed laity should see it as a privilege
and an opportunity to stage the major festivals, as well as to
conduct weddings and funerals. When it comes to synodical
government, the law leaves us no choice but to draw up an
electoral roll. But discretion is probably the wisest course:
distribute the forms to the committed members, while not
mentioning this awkward democratic process to the parish
as a whole! Alternatively, distribute the forms like confetti,
allowing anybody to pick one up and fill it in.

There remains the knotty issue of baptism, over which
such intense and destructive emotions can arise. The worst
of all worlds is for the vicar to baptise the children of 'Old
Testament members', while insisting that they first jump
over various hurdles, such as attending a course or coming
to church for a month. This creates resentment, without in
any way advancing the Gospel. If a clergyman, as a matter
of conscience, feels that only the children of committed
church-goers (the 'New Testament members') should be
baptised, then he should say so clearly; people may dis-
agree, but they will respect his position. Those who do not
hold such a high view should baptise the children of anyone
who asks. This strictly is what the law requires. More
importantly, baptism can quite properly be regarded as
part of Old Testament religion. After all, when John first
baptised people in the River Jordan, Jesus had not yet
appeared; immersion in water was a ritual which prepared
people to receive the Saviour – as does all good folk religion.

WHAT ABOUT THE DIFFERENT
DENOMINATIONS?

An Anglican clergyman, who had been serving in an ecumenical team in a large Hertfordshire town, went to be
vicar of a group of four villages in Leicestershire. Within

his new parishes there were no Roman Catholic or Nonconformist churches, although one of the villages had a Methodist chapel which twenty years earlier had been turned into
a house, and in another village the old Baptist chapel had
become the village hall. The vicar was filled with ecumenical zeal, and soon after he arrived he inquired whether
there had ever been any ecumenical services in the parishes.
The people responded with polite incomprehension, not
knowing what an ecumenical service was. But he rightly
surmised that there must be some Catholics, Methodists
and Baptists living within the villages. So in late January
he decided to hold the service specified for the Week of
Prayer for Christian Unity, in the hope of 'flushing out'
the other denominations. He put up posters and circulated
a leaflet to every house advertising the event.

When he emerged from the vestry door at the start of
the service he was initially pleased to see the church filled
with people. But during the first hymn, as he looked round
at the faces, he was disheartened to realise that the congregation consisted entirely of his regular church-goers from
the four villages. At the end of the service he asked why
no one from any other denominations had come. 'You're
wrong, vicar', came the reply; 'Betty over there is Methodist, Henry and Margaret are Baptists, Nora is Roman
Catholic . . .' and so the list went on. To his surprise
he found that his regular congregations were already
ecumenical.

Without any deliberate intention, and often without
being aware, our village churches have for many decades
been in the forefront of the ecumenical movement. As the
Nonconformist churches have closed in rural areas, so
many of their old members have started attending the
parish churches; and newcomers to a village who have a
Nonconformist background will usually prefer to worship
at the parish church with their neighbours, than travel five

or ten miles to the nearest town on Sunday morning. Roman Catholic parishes in rural areas typically cover twenty, forty or even sixty villages, with the church located in the local market town. Many Catholics who move to the countryside are willing and able to travel to their church for Mass. But some, especially the elderly without transport, take a deep breath, and cross the threshold of the Anglican church in their village. And with a little encouragement from the vicar or minister in charge they may even start receiving Communion. Moreover, in most villages all the devout Catholics happily come to the festivals which do not involve the Eucharist, such as harvest and Christmas carols.

This easy-going attitude to denominational differences goes right back to the Reformation. While the great majority of clergy and laity accepted and even welcomed the break from Rome under Henry VIII, a small number of families, belonging mainly to the aristocracy, remained loyal to the Pope. These recusants, as they were known, suffered intermittent persecution, which reached a climax after Guy Fawkes's abortive attempt to blow up parliament. In the remote countryside, however, relations were mostly cordial. If the squire and his family chose to remain Catholic, neither the vicar nor his congregation were unduly perturbed. Indeed, any squire who took his faith so seriously was likely also to be generous to the poor, and even set his rents low. In one famous case a Catholic lady, the Duchess of Lennox, paid for the restoration of an Anglican parish church, Leighton Bromswold, whose prebendary was the great poet George Herbert; and while building work proceeded she allowed services to be held in her manor house.

To most country people the bitter religious quarrels of the sixteenth and seventeenth centuries seemed remote and irrelevant. Even at the height of the Middle Ages few country churches could afford the fine silver, the elaborate vestments and the glorious stained glass of the cathedrals and urban churches. Instead, the worship was simple and unfussy and, apart from a few paintings on the walls, there was little decoration. So when the Protestant reformers sought to rid the Church of England of papist 'idolatry', there were numerous statues and windows to smash in the cities while in many villages a coat of whitewash was sufficient.

Similarly, the rural clergy had little difficulty in adapting to the new ways. Their Latin was mostly poor, so they were relieved to lead worship in English; and slight adjustments to their liturgical dress rarely caused anxiety. As for theology, it is doubtful whether many understood the issues about which bishops and dons were prepared to die at the stake. So it is hardly surprising that in many country parishes the same clergymen remained in post throughout the turbulent middle years of the sixteenth century, turning Protestant under Henry, reverting to Catholicism under Mary, and becoming Protestant again under Elizabeth. Likewise many country parsons survived unscathed when Charles I was defeated by Cromwell, and again when the monarchy was restored under Charles II. The evidence for this clerical tranquillity can be seen in the list of incumbents which can be found in most churches: observe how infrequently the parson changes in the late 1530s, in 1553, in 1558, in the late 1640s, and in 1660 – all dates when officially the Anglican Church underwent radical change.

The picture does, however, become somewhat bleaker in the period after the Restoration. With the approval of the new king, the bishops sought to eradicate all Puritan influence from the church of England, with the result that many Puritans felt compelled to break from the national church and form their own independent congregations. In the following century the Evangelical movement led to a further

split. The bone of contention was not doctrine, but organisation. While many Evangelicals felt able to conduct their
missions within the parochial framework, others, including
John Wesley, believed that this inhibited the spreading of
the Gospel. Wesley and others began forming local religious
societies with their own lay preachers to organise public
lectures and prayer meetings. Not surprisingly many
incumbents, including some with Evangelical leanings, felt
that their authority was being undermined, and objected
strongly. Finally, after Wesley's death, these societies severed all ties with the Church of England to form the Methodist Church.

Thus by the early nineteenth century many villages had
a Methodist chapel and a Baptist meeting-house in addition
to the parish church. In some parts of the country, such as
Devon and Cornwall, the split between church and chapel
divided the villages politically and socially, as well as spiritually. The squire and his tenants and servants attended
the parish church and voted Tory, while the artisans and
the yeomen farmers belonged to one or other of the chapels,
and voted Liberal. Indeed, the continuing strength of Lib-
eralism in the West Country owes its origins to the rise of
Nonconformity.

Within living memory competition between Anglicanism
and Nonconformity was in many villages extremely fierce.
Parson and minister vied with each other in attracting the
village children to their Sunday Schools, even offering
sweets and special outings as 'bribes', and everyone was
acutely aware of the relative numbers attending church
and chapel. But in the last fifty years or so, for reasons
that are hard to fathom, Nonconformity has retreated with
astonishing haste from the countryside while the Church
of England has held its ground. By the 1950s and 1960s
chapels in village after village were being closed down, as
their congregations dwindled to a demoralised handful.

Today the Methodist or Baptist chapel has become a rarity in rural England, so that Nonconformity has become almost exclusively urban.

One cannot help but feel sad at the sight of so many fine Nonconformist chapels, built with the hard-earned pennies of local craftsmen and labourers, turned into private residences, their former austere glory lost beneath bright wallpaper and fitted carpets. Yet spiritually the decline of Nonconformity has wrought a miracle of Christian unity, and actually increased church attendance.

The Methodists, Baptists and Congregationalists who tentatively try out the parish church are often surprised at how quickly they feel at home. They may have been to a suburban Anglican church, and felt somewhat repelled by what (to their eyes) seemed excessive fuss up in the chancel. The simple services of rural Anglicanism can, however, seem much more homely. More importantly, the old-fashioned worship of many country churches embodies the common traditions of all English Christians, both Protestant and Catholic. As we shall explore later, Cranmer and his associates tried to include the best elements of medieval Catholic worship in their new Prayer Book, and succeeded in adapting medieval worship to make it acceptable to the most ardent Puritan. Sadly, in the mid-seventeenth century the Prayer Book became a bone of contention between the High Churchmen and the Puritans, with some Puritans wanting to abandon it altogether; but despite this, many Nonconformists to this day happily incorporate large chunks of the Prayer Book in their worship. Those Puritans and Evangelicals who remained loyal to the Church of England regarded the Prayer Book as the foundation of godly worship, bitterly criticising the lax clergymen who did not follow its rubrics to the letter.

The old-fashioned hymn-books, still widely used in country churches, also embody our common tradition. In this case it was initially Nonconformists like Isaac Watt who pioneered English hymnody; and when by the early nineteenth century the Anglicans started to catch up, they happily included Nonconformist hymns in their compilations. Then in the late nineteenth century the musical traffic flowed the other way, with the best Anglican hymns finding their way into Nonconformist hymn-books. More recently, as Roman Catholics have discovered the pleasures of hymn-singing, they have freely adopted both Anglican and Nonconformist hymns. Thus when Baptists, Methodists or Catholics pick up *Hymns Ancient and Modern* (which is by far the most common hymn-book in rural areas) they find themselves familiar with a large proportion of the contents.

In economic affairs competition is usually beneficial, supplying the consumer with better products at lower prices. In spiritual affairs, by contrast, opposite laws seem to apply. As recent studies have confirmed, in villages where there is still a Nonconformist chapel, the total number of practising Christians is usually less than in villages which have only the parish church. In part this is because rivalry between churches undoubtedly mars their Christian witness – Jesus, after all, came to preach love and unity, praying that 'all may be one' – but it is also because the church flourishes best in a village where it is felt to be the heart of the community, embodying its common values. Thus where there is a single church, people will be more inclined to attend its services, both out of commitment to Christ, and as an expression of social solidarity.

We should not, of course, exaggerate the ecumenical virtues of the country church. There are many Nonconformists who find its worship dull and stodgy, particularly if they are accustomed to more demonstrative styles of worship. Equally, there are some country churches which in the past century have adopted some of the 'fussy' habits of the urban church, and thus lost the austere simplicity which can have such a broad appeal in Britain. Yet numerous villages which have remained true to their spiritual roots have, in recent decades, made great ecumenical strides, overtaking even the most daring suburban experiments in Christian unity. Thus in considering questions of ministry and worship we must beware of jeopardising this achievement, but instead seek to learn lessons from it, and in the process rural Christianity may have valuable lessons to teach the church as a whole.

2

WORSHIP

IS SMALL BEAUTIFUL?

Village churches vary enormously in scale. Some almost
rival cathedrals, with a long nave, transepts to the north
and south, and a grand chancel at the east end. Others are
no bigger than a farmhouse, so that the English habit of
leaving the front pews empty is frustrated if more than a
handful come to a service. It is commonly imagined that
the size of the church reflects the village's population in
medieval times. More probably it is a tribute to the wealth
and devotion of the lord of the manor — those huge village
churches were never full, even at Christmas immediately
prior to the Black Death. Certainly today there is almost
no correlation between the number of potential worshippers
and the number of pews.

Yet if we can make no generalisation about the size of
buildings, we can about the size of congregation. On an
average Sunday in an average village church the congregation is small. In a typical hamlet with a population of
less than two hundred, the number of worshippers is probably in single figures, and may even be a literal expression
of Christ's dictum about 'two or three gathered together'.
A large village of around a thousand souls may have twenty
or even thirty in church, but there are many such villages
which also have single-figure congregations.

This does not mean, as casual observers sometimes suggest, that the rural church is dying on its feet. Or, if it does, the urban church is at its last gasp. Estimates vary, but the best guess is that on a typical Sunday between one and two per cent of the urban population attends church; while in rural areas the figure is around twice as high. But four per cent church attendance in a village of one hundred and fifty souls means only six worshippers, while one per cent in an urban parish of ten thousand yields a congregation of a hundred.

For many clergy, and also for many newcomers to village life, small congregations are a source of profound anxiety and even spiritual depression. They are probably accustomed to a bustling parish communion, in which the nave is at least half full, and the chancel swirls with choristers and servers in pretty robes. There are rotas of laypeople to read the lesson and lead the intercessions, and every month the Sunday School children enthral the adults with a short play illustrating a Bible story. Understandably, anyone accustomed to such a rich spiritual diet feels starved when they start attending a country church. The main Sunday service in a village seems to the newcomer similar to the early-morning Communion in a town, which for most people provides insufficient spiritual calories.

In recent years a number of rural clergy have tried to recreate the urban style of worship by treating their group of churches as a single parish. On Sunday morning they have a single major service, usually in the form of a parish communion, which is held in a different church each week. Thus if a parson has four churches in his case, each plays host to the parish communion once a month, and the people are asked to travel to a neighbouring village three times a month. In some dioceses, such as Lincoln and Hereford, where as many as eight or ten parishes have a single clergyman, people may sometimes be asked to travel as far as ten miles to receive the sacrament.

To the clergyman who feels that Sunday worship requires a large congregation, this arrangement seems ideal. Moreover, it saves him from dashing from one church to another on Sunday morning, and instead enables him to have coffee with his people after the service. But while in some places it seems to work well, in most groups of parishes the average number of worshippers drops significantly. Many people simply refuse to travel, even if transport is provided, and only attend worship when the parish communion is held in their village. Indeed, some clergy find that, after an initial effort at travelling, almost everyone gives up, so he finds himself ministering to an entirely different congregation each week. In effect, therefore, the arrangement is merely a ploy to reduce his work-load!

The clergyman may rant and rave in the privacy of his vicarage at his people's stubbornness, but there are good reasons for their behaviour. The groups into which villages are put are usually quite arbitrary, dreamt up by bishops and archdeacons, largely for administrative convenience; and over the years a village may have found itself in three or four different groups. So the parishioners are wary of any pressure from the parson to pool their spiritual efforts, let alone pool the collections. More fundamentally, the congregations understand quite clearly that they exist as part of the village community, and that their attendance at worship is an expression of their mutual commitment, as well as their commitment to God. The travelling parish communion thus destroys a vital element in their worship. Sadly, too many clergy have found themselves locked in bitter conflict with their people on this issue, leaving a dark stain of suspicion which is very hard to erase. Indeed, some clergy, after such rows, have concluded that, as soon as is decently possible, they will apply for an urban parish.

Yet if one stands back from the rural scene, one can see a strange paradox over the question of size. The profession which is probably closest to that of parochial ministry is teaching, and among teachers and lecturers small classes are a dream which only rarely is realised. They rightly believe that their work would be both more effective and more enjoyable if they had fewer pupils. Indeed, to most teachers a class of around ten or a dozen children would be ideal, while lecturers at university prefer tutorial groups of two or three students. It is worth asking why smaller groups work better in education, and whether the same factors may apply in worship. There are at least three good reasons for small classes.

The first and most obvious is that the personal relationship between teacher and pupil can be much stronger in a small group. The teacher is more aware of the particular problems and needs of the pupil, and thence can adapt the style and method of teaching to respond to those needs. Equally, the pupil generally works better for a teacher who is known and loved. The second is that the teacher can be more natural and relaxed. In a large class or lecture theatre the teacher must, to some degree, put on a performance, projecting his or her voice and personality in order to hold the pupil's attention. In a small group the teacher can talk at a normal level and act in a normal way, and thence enjoy an easy and comfortable rapport with the class. The third is that in a small class shy pupils are more willing to speak, contributing to classroom discussion, whereas in a large group a small number of extrovert pupils tend to dominate lessons while the rest remain silent.   .

All these advantages of small classes in school apply equally to small congregations in church. In a country church the minister soon gets to know all the regular churchgoers quite intimately; and if he or she stays in the same place for ten years or more, the bonds can become almost as strong as those within a family. Thus when they gather for the service on Sunday it is a meeting of close friends. This can enhance the quality of the worship greatly. When prayers are said together, hearts as well as voices are speaking in unison to God. When there is a piece of dialogue in the liturgy, such as the *Sursum Corda* in the Communion ('Lift up your hearts . . .') and the Responses in Matins and Evensong ('O Lord, open thou our lips . . .'), it can be experienced as a real spiritual conversation. Even the liturgical greeting – 'The Lord be with you'; 'And with thy spirit' – can feel like a pleasant expression of good wishes, as occurs when village people meet each other in the street.

The personal intimacy between parson and people also enables the parson to adapt the details of worship in response to personal needs and circumstances. A favourite hymn can be chosen for someone's birthday or a couple's wedding anniversary. People may feel able to mention to the parson just before the service friends and relatives for whom they would like prayers to be offered. When the notices are given there can be an opportunity for the parson and others to mention any village news that is appropriate, such as the condition of sick parishioners, or the name of anyone who has recently moved into the village. In preparing his sermon the parson can also bear in mind the particular concerns of those likely to be listening, as well as avoiding points that might cause unnecessary hurt or offence.

It is often said that clergymen tend to be failed actors – although, as Laurence Olivier once remarked, it can equally be said that many actors are failed clergymen! – and for the more histrionic parson a large suburban congregation provides a perfect forum for his talents. But there are numerous excellent clergymen who have no dramatic skills, and who thus find it extremely stressful to project their voice and personality to a hundred or more people. Happily, such clerical shyness and reserve suits the countryside admirably. Blood-warming oratory to a congregation of half a dozen is manifestly absurd; indeed, one suspects that our most famous preachers, such as Billy Graham, would be at a loss for words in a village church. A quiet, natural approach, however, in which the parson conducts the service in the same tone and volume that he uses in ordinary conversation, is ideal for the countryside.

A large congregation may be blessed with an abundance of men and women willing to read the lesson, lead prayers, deliver notices and take other public roles in worship. Yet these inevitably are the more extrovert members of the church, while the introvert majority remain silent. In a village church there may at first sight seem a dearth of people to perform such tasks, each person expressing anxious modesty about their fitness to do more than hand out hymn-books and take the collection. But with a little cajoling even quite shy and nervous people can be persuaded to read the epistle or lead intercessions. When they have succeeded in plucking up courage they are often astonished to discover that such simple actions feel like a genuine offering to God. Moreover, in small congregations all the worshippers can have a turn every month or two.

There is, however, one seemingly trivial matter that can undermine all the advantages of smallness: the places in which people sit. In a surprising number of rural churches electric heaters have been put under the back three rows of pews, while leaving the front rows cold. As the church-wardens may argue, people sit only at the back, so heaters at the front would be a waste of money. The consequence, of course, is a vast empty zone between parson and people, thus making nonsense of any attempt to establish a personal rapport, and forcing the parson to declaim, rather than speak, the service. The larger the church building, the more acute this problem is likely to be: it is not unknown for twenty or thirty yards to separate the clergyman at the altar from his nearest parishioner.

It is a sound investment, spiritually and materially, to scrap the heaters at the back, and heat only the front pews. After initial grumbling the laity will be pleasantly surprised at how much more they enjoy worship; and, if worship is more satisfying, in the fullness of time more people will come – and the increased collections will pay for the new heaters! Incidentally, one needs to watch for people retreating to the back pews in summer – this peculiarly English vice is hard to eradicate.

IS OLD BEAUTIFUL?

In recent years it has been fashionable to conduct 'village appraisals', in which a questionnaire is circulated to every household, asking opinions on everything from the quality of the local bus service to the colour of the village hall paint. There is usually a section marked 'Religion', in which views on worship are solicited; and often people are asked whether they prefer the old service in the Book of Common Prayer, or the new services in the Alternative Service Book. To the chagrin of many modern-minded vicars, Cranmer gains in most villages between eighty and ninety per cent support. This overwhelming vote of confidence has been confirmed in national surveys of rural opinion.

In most urban parishes the battle between the old and new services is over, at least for the time being. The Communion has been conducted in modern language for almost two decades, so that many church-goers today have never heard Cranmer's majestic phrases. Admittedly older parishioners may recall bitter disputes on the Parochial Church Council when the vicar first introduced the new services, but the opponents have long since left the church, died, or simply swallowed their objections.

In the countryside, by contrast, the issue remains unresolved, and is still keenly felt. Country parsons have tended to be older than their urban brethren, so in the 1970s they were often less enthusiastic about the new services. Moreover, those who move to the countryside, as well as those born and bred there, tend to be more conservative in their attitudes and tastes. As a result the current picture is very confused. In some parishes the clergyman has insisted on using the modern services, to the total exclusion of Cranmer; more commonly an uneasy compromise has been reached, in which the old and new awkwardly rub shoulders. A not untypical arrangement is for the Book of Common Prayer to be used for Communion on the first Sunday of the month, and for Evensong on the third Sunday; while on the second and fourth Sundays the Alternative Service Book is followed. In surprisingly few rural parishes, given the strong preference for Cranmer, the modern services have been spurned altogether.

This muddle satisfies almost no one. Left to themselves there is little doubt that most country parishes would revert to an exclusive diet of Cranmer, locking those brightly-coloured modern booklets in the vestry cupboard. But most clergy today, and a significant minority of newcomers, strongly prefer the Alternative Service Book. Indeed, many younger clergy have little or no experience of the Book of Common Prayer, either at theological college or in the parishes where they served as curates, and they have probably been taught that the modern services are theologically more sound, and historically based on an earlier foundation. The fact that the modern services are so widely used in the countryside is almost entirely due to clerical pressure.

The deal that so many parishes have struck, in which

old and new are used on alternate Sundays, seems at first sight the most sensible answer. After all, parson and people say to themselves, the British excel in the art of compromise. Yet, as they soon come to realise, this leaves them with the worst of all worlds. Devotees of Cranmer may skip the services they dislike; and even those who come to all the services experience difficulty in finding their way about two such different service books. As is often remarked, 'Roman Catholics attend church in order to find God, while Anglicans attend church to find the page number!' To the new church-goer, tentatively trying out Christian worship, the situation is even more dire. Faced with such complexity many retreat in despair, concluding that Anglican services can only be tackled with the aid of a computer. Although it is too early to be certain, there is already evidence that parishes which adopt such a compromise condemn themselves to a long, slow death: old church-goers either leave immediately in disgust or eventually take their place in the churchyard, while potential new church-goers are deterred.

The general arguments – theological, aesthetic and historical – over the old and new services have been rehearsed in great detail during the past quarter of a century. Certainly the modern services are more in tune with current theological attitudes, putting, for example, less emphasis on sin and guilt, and giving greater prominence to forgiveness and joy; but in a world faced with such enormous moral and political problems, some feel that the sterner tones of Cranmer are more appropriate. The language of the modern services is undoubtedly easier to understand; but few dispute the awesome beauty of Cranmer's phrases. We are assured that Rite A in the Alternative Service Book is firmly rooted in the earliest liturgy which scholars can find, dating from the third century; but equally it can be argued that the Book of Common Prayer has its roots in

English culture, and is thus more congenial to the English mind.

Setting all these higher concerns to one side, however, we should ask whether there are issues that relate specifically to the countryside. In particular, we should ask the people themselves who so strongly support Cranmer to explain their reasons.

The word which most quickly comes to their lips is 'continuity'. The Book of Common Prayer has been used for over four centuries in the village churches of England, impregnating their solid stone walls with its words and rhythms. Thus to repeat those same words and rhythms is to enter a stream of prayer that has carried countless generations through 'the changes and chances of this mortal life'. This desire for continuity is based not on intellectual belief, but on emotional conviction, which has grown stronger rather than weaker in recent decades. As the pace of change in the world has quickened, so the ancient village church has become a symbol of stability, offering comfort and reassurance; and to many of those who choose to move from city to village this symbol is especially powerful. When the village church echoes to the liturgy of Cranmer the reassurance is complete – and when modern services are used it can cause profound offence.

Many clergy, as well as a few lay people, reply that this attachment to ancient buildings and services is a form of escapism, in which the worshipper is using Christianity as a shield against the modern world, and any country minister who knows his or her people well must recognise some truth in this charge. In particular, some of the professional newcomers seem to lead a double life, pursuing in their bustling city offices all sorts of 'devices and desires', for which in the tranquil village church they ask forgiveness. Yet such an abuse of faith does not itself condemn this impulse for continuity and tradition. Jesus himself was deeply versed in the ancient prayers of Judaism, quoting their resonant phrases in his own prayers, and he urged his disciples also to remain loyal to their traditions, knowing that only by being firmly rooted in the past could they face the challenges of the future. At its best the rural devotion to the old prayer book stems from this same insight, in which tradition is maintained as a source of courage.

A second word which springs readily to the lips of Cranmer's defenders is 'mystery'. People often imagine that in the sixteenth century ordinary people spoke in the language and rhythms of the Book of Common Prayer, so that the meaning was transparently clear. In fact, Cranmer and the other compilers deliberately chose a highly literary and poetic style of English, in order to conjure a sense of awe and grandeur. Arguably, in the man-made environment of the city, in which human reason is supposed to rule, such liturgical poetry jars; so the more literal language of the modern services is more appropriate. But amid the fields and copses of the countryside, faith is best expressed in sonorous cadences and harmonious metaphors. Indeed, at a time when we need to defend the natural beauty of the countryside and conserve its ecological balance, poetic liturgy gains even greater power.

A third, and perhaps unexpected, word often applied to the Book of Common Prayer is 'brevity'. If the initial exhortations are excluded, Cranmer's Holy Communion service, with five hymns and a short sermon, takes no longer than forty-five minutes. Rite A in the Alternative Service Book, with its long intercessions and even longer Eucharistic Prayer, adds an extra ten minutes. In a cold country church this can make the difference between mild discomfort and positive pain! Besides, with a small congregation a short, simple service feels more natural. Indeed, surprising as it may seem, Rite A can sound almost pompous in a country church.

The fourth and final word which village people use about Cranmer is 'formality'. This, too may appear odd, since a small, intimate congregation hardly requires stiff politeness in its worship. Yet, paradoxically, the informality which can bring such joy to urban worship is required precisely because people do not know each well. The hand-shaking at the Peace, and even hand-clapping during the more jolly hymns, can break down barriers, and generate a warm sense of fellowship even among total strangers. In a rural congregation, by contrast, such gestures can seem both unnecessary and artificial. There is ample opportunity for warm fellowship in the village street or over cups of tea in each others' homes. When it comes to Sunday worship this warmth can be taken for granted, so people can simply relax together, in calm tranquillity, before God. To the newcomer (including the new vicar) their behaviour in church may seem like cold indifference to each other; in fact, the opposite is usually true.

Continuity, mystery, brevity and formality – these do not in themselves make a compelling case for preserving the Book of Common Prayer in our rural churches, and undoubtedly there are some villages where Rite A or Rite B is most appropriate. But they do carry considerable emotional and spiritual weight, and the eager clergyman would be wise to listen carefully to these deeply-held convictions before enacting radical changes. Nevertheless, sticking to Cranmer does not mean imprisoning oneself in a liturgical strait-jacket: new styles of music can be explored – indeed, as we shall see, guitars and recorders are more in keeping with the worship of Cranmer than the heavy nineteenth-century organ – and a lively, punchy sermon, filled with topical illustrations, would also bring pleasure to Cranmer's ears.

There is in addition one technical innovation which is worth considering. One of the major objections to the Book of Common Prayer is that to the modern eye the layout is extremely confusing. Moreover, since large chunks are usually left out, worshippers can find themselves constantly fumbling to find their place. It is not hard to extract the relevant parts, and print them on a leaflet. The congregational prayers in the Communion can easily be fitted on to a folded A4 card, as can the main canticles and prayers of Matins and Evensong. Those who wish to use the books can still do so, while the rest can be saved a great deal of anxiety. Incidentally, copyright permission should first be sought – simply write to the address given on the flyleaf of the modern edition of the Book of Common Prayer.

HOW CAN A HANDFUL SING HYMNS?

Current disputes about old and new services are like the proverbial vicarage tea parties compared with the disputes in the last century over music. For centuries the psalms and hymns had been accompanied by the village orchestra, consisting of four or five ordinary folk who could play an instrument – a fiddle, clarinet, a recorder and anything else that came to hand. They were paid a small fee, and for some this was their main, or even their only, source of income. They were not always fine exemplars of Christian living; and, like the bell-ringers, they were occasionally drunk by the time of Evensong on Sunday afternoon, so the psalm chants sounded somewhat wonky. But to squire and peasant alike the village orchestra was part of the fabric of rural life, whose existence one never thought to question.

Yet by the 1830s and 1840s a growing number of clergy were convinced that such motley bands of players were not fit for divine worship. The Evangelical movement, which had been sweeping across Britain for over half a century, had made the clergy far less tolerant of moral laxity within the church, so drunkenness and revelry among musicians and bell-ringers were no longer regarded with benign amusement, but seen as an offence against the Almighty. The Tractarian Movement, which blew like a gale through Britain after 1833, encouraged clergy to despise the simple, unaffected style of the normal village service, and taught them to aspire to the highest standards of cathedral worship in every parish church: and since cathedrals have grand organs and robed choirs, so the zealous parson sought to introduce an organ and choir into his church.

George Eliot, in *Scenes from Clerical Life*, describes the numb horror with which these innovations were greeted. Not only did people object to these musical pretensions, but they were shocked that many clergymen could drive the old musicians into destitution without even a twinge of conscience. However, as with the introduction of modern services in our own time, the clergy won the day. By the 1870s most larger villages had installed double-manual pipe organs, at huge expense, and smaller villages had purchased the best harmonium they could afford. In addition a set of robes were bought, and stalls put on either side of the chancel, so that the feeble croaks of the congregation could be uplifted by a choir.

Yet, for all its virtues in a cathedral and a large urban church, the organ is far from ideal in a village. A full-scale pipe organ is too loud for a small congregation, who find themselves singing against it, rather than with it. An organ is also expensive to maintain and repair which, to a village struggling to keep the church itself in good order, can breed considerable resentment. As many country parishes have discovered, appeals for the organ elicit more grumbles than money and, to add insult to injury, many rural churches today do not have among their congregations anyone who is willing and able to play the instrument. They are thus faced with the grim choice of paying an organist out of their meagre funds, or of abandoning the organ altogether. The sad consequence is that in some smaller village churches hymn-singing is dying out, revived only at harvest and Christmas.

Going back beyond the introduction of the organ, congregational singing has been central to English worship since the Reformation in the sixteenth century. Throughout the medieval period Christian music had been confined to cathedrals and monasteries, where choirs sang the most exquisite plainchant, while any laity present remained silent. Cranmer and the other English reformers sought to bring every aspect of traditional worship, including music, within the reach of ordinary people, so in the decades following the publication of Cranmer's Prayer Book numerous people, including Queen Elizabeth I, set about composing metrical psalms. These consisted of taking one of the psalms in the Bible, rewriting it in the form of a ballad, and setting it to a popular melody. Lay people were thus delighted to find themselves in church singing tunes familiar from the local tavern, but with the old ribald words replaced by holy verses. Of these early metrical psalms we retain only one with both its words and tune unchanged, 'All people that on earth do dwell', but we still sing the words of many metrical psalms set to newer tunes, such as 'The Lord's my Shepherd', and 'As pants the hart'.

The Evangelicals of the eighteenth century soon realised the power of popular singing as a tool of mission, and men like Charles Wesley (John's younger brother) and Philip Doddridge also took popular tunes, familiar from the streets and taverns, and set Christian words to them. But instead of confining themselves to the psalms, they felt free to write original verses, expressing their own spiritual insights and sentiments. Thousands upon thousands of such hymns were composed, and could be heard down mines, in factories and in fields, as ordinary men and women who had been touched by Evangelical preaching celebrated their faith. At first Anglican parsons were suspicious, fearing that these new-fangled Christian songs could undermine the dignity of their services. By the early nineteenth century, however, they had realised that the Evangelicals were merely extending a musical tradition initiated by Cranmer, and soon High Churchmen like Keble, Newman and Faber were composing stirring hymns of their own.

When small village churches consider their music nowadays, the history of English hymnody offers valuable encouragement. Hymns are folk music; in fact, they are the most flourishing form of folk music in Britain today. Many of the tunes we still sing are based on folk melodies that were handed down through countless generations, and even those that were written by professional composers are for the most part rooted in the folk idiom. Moreover, about twenty or thirty hymns form part of our common cultural furniture, known by everyone: 'Abide with me', 'Onward, Christian Soldiers', 'O God, our help in ages past', 'When I survey the wondrous cross', 'All things bright and beautiful' – we could all complete the list.

Congregational hymnody is thus quite distinct from cathedral music, which is rooted in the monastic and the classical traditions. Admittedly there is considerable borrowing from one tradition to another: such popular standards as 'Thine be the glory' and 'Let all mortal flesh keep silence' belong respectively to the classical and the monastic idioms. But the attempt by nineteenth-century clergy to apply the standards of the cathedral to the ordinary parish church has been, to say the least, a mixed blessing, and within the village, which is the home of our folk music, it has been little short of a disaster. Small rural congregations cannot begin to match the choral standards of a suburban parish, let alone a cathedral, so they are condemned to regard themselves as musical failures; and, not surprisingly, newcomers to the village church often complain, above all things, of the dreariness of the hymn-singing.

Manifestly, the solution is to adopt once again the musical attitudes of our seventeenth- and eighteenth-century forbears. To start with, select only those hymns which are pleasant and easy to sing. Too many clergy waste precious hours in choosing hymns whose words seem to fit the theme of the Bible readings given for that Sunday; or, worse still, they choose adventurous tunes which the choir in their former parish especially enjoyed. On the contrary, rural hymn-singing should be unashamedly populist – applying the standards of Radios 1 and 2, not 3 and 4 – and the way to discover which are the most popular hymns is simply to ask people. The new country parson can win considerable trust if, within a few months of his arrival, he asks all the regular church-goers to write down their forty favourite hymns. There will be much overlap between lists; but by this means he will gain a list of between eighty and a hundred true Christian folk songs. He may from this list try to fit hymns to weekly themes; but better to belt out God's praise in a familiar, inappropriate hymn, than to mumble his praise in the correct words.

On the face of it such shameless populism seems to preclude innovation. Yet folk music is kept alive by being open and absorbent, and within the past few decades at least a dozen new hymns have passed into the popular canon, such as 'Lord of all hopefulness', 'Morning has broken', 'Lord of the Dance' and 'Tell out my soul'. Indeed, rural clergy who have asked their congregations to list their favourite hymns have been surprised to find such modern hymns high up in the hit parade. People are always happy to try out a new hymn with an attractive tune: if after three or four plays it catches on, add it to the list; if not, drop it. The moral is to trust popular taste – that is what folk music is all about.

Sadly, none of the hymn-books currently on the market really suit the rural church. *Hymns Ancient and Modern* remains the best; but unfortunately the selection of modern hymns contained in the New Standard edition is too high-brow. *Mission Praise*, despite its many virtues, is aimed at large congregations, especially those of Evangelical or Charismatic inclination. The new Roman Catholic hymnals are probably the best, but they exclude a number of old Anglican favourites. None the less, this dearth can be turned to an advantage. A group of rural parishes can derive great pleasure from compiling its own hymn-book, using small ring binders. Using a modern word processor and a good printer, both the words and melody of each hymn can be typed on to an A5 sheet and photocopied. New hymns can then be added at will. Incidentally, if author or composer is still alive, or has died within the last fifty years, copyright permission should be sought.

A church with an organ in working order, and an organist willing to play it, would be well advised simply to count its blessings. But if the organ is defunct, or there is no organist, this should be seized on as a God-given opportunity to revive the village orchestra. A remarkable number of men and women under the age of forty can strum a guitar, and even more were taught to play the recorder at school. Guitars and recorders comprise a quite adequate orchestra; and, if a violin, flute, clarinet or even drums can be added, so much the better. If the congregation lacks any players, it may be possible to persuade someone with a musical ear to take up the guitar, which within a few months can be mastered sufficiently to accompany hymns. A guitar providing the rhythm and harmony, plus a strong voice to lead the singing, is perfectly satisfactory.

Such simple instruments are ideal for small congre-

gations. As few as two or three people can sing happily
together with such an accompaniment – with an organ
their voices would be drowned. They will also discover that
some hymns are actually better suited to such treatment,
especially the old metrical psalms. For example, 'All people
that on earth do dwell' is usually sung as a solemn dirge,
with the organ thumping out a ponderous harmony. If,
however, it is sung at twice the usual speed, with the light
backing of guitar and recorder, it becomes a delightful
carol. That other funereal psalm, 'O God, our help in ages
past', is also transformed by such treatment, its easy lilt
echoing Time's 'ever-rolling stream'.

At the harvest festival and the Christmas carol service it
is worth trawling the entire village for players. Violins and
cellos can be taken from lofts and dusted down; flutes and
clarinets can be reassembled; and the children can bring
triangles and tambourines. There is no better way of drawing people to church than filling the chancel with
an impromptu orchestra with each family in the village
represented.

HOW DOES ONE PREACH TO A HANDFUL?

Of all the elements in our worship, the sermon has over
the centuries generated the greatest anxiety. The great
controversies over the meaning and frequency of Holy
Communion were largely confined to clergy and theologians, but the substance and length of the sermon have
been matters of dispute and worry for clergy and laity
alike. Happily, the sermon has also been the focus of wry
amusement – witness P. G. Wodehouse's 'Great Sermon
Handicap'.

The medieval country priest rarely, if ever, preached a
sermon. He might never even have read the Bible, let

alone studied it in sufficient depth to expound its meaning. Instead, his congregation relied for their religious knowledge on the brightly-coloured pictures which covered the walls of the church, illustrating the main Bible stories and the lives of the saints. The Protestant reformers quite rightly regarded this situation as extremely unsatisfactory, and made the training of ministers an urgent priority. By the late sixteenth century the sermon was firmly entrenched in the pattern of Sunday worship.

Unfortunately, the style of preaching soon became a bone of contention between the Puritans and High Churchmen. The Puritans regarded the sermon as the centre of worship, and believed that it should last at least an hour, if not two or even three hours. Indeed, hourglasses were manufactured (like large egg-timers), which stood on a special stand next to the pulpit, and as each hour passed the minister ceremoniously turned the hourglass over. Moreover, the minister was expected to preach, and the laity expected to listen to, two such sermons each Sunday, one in the morning and the other in the late afternoon. The Puritan sermon was usually a detailed commentary on a particular passage, or even a single verse, of the Bible, and its explicit aim was 'conversion', so that by the end of the spiritual marathon each Sunday the laity would have turned anew to Christ.

The High Churchmen by contrast saw the sermon as one feature in a service whose main purpose was prayer and adoration. Many High Churchmen continued the medieval practice of weekly Communion, slotting a sermon, lasting ten or fifteen minutes, after the Creed. Indeed, this practice was clearly intended by Cranmer himself, since the Communion is the only service in which the preaching of a sermon is specified. Others, however, had been sufficiently influenced by Puritan attitudes to have full Communion only once a month, using the Ante-Communion (the first part of the service) combined with Matins on other Sundays. But here too the sermon remained quite short, and the parson was allowed to range quite widely, reflecting on general moral and spiritual questions as well as expounding Scripture.

After the Restoration in 1660 the sermon went into decline with the Church of England, although, of course, it was maintained in all its Puritan glory in the Nonconformist churches. The laity who had laboured under Puritan parsons were for the most part delighted to be free of lengthy sermonising, and free also of the strict rules against sports and pleasures on the Sabbath. So Sunday became, as it had been in medieval times, a day for enjoyment and recreation. After the rather brief Morning Service was over, cricket and football were played on the village green (in a somewhat less orderly form than our modern versions), and ale flowed in the taverns. Since the parson himself often shared these revels, he was only too glad to cut his sermon to a minimum. The habit thus developed (which has dogged Anglican sermons ever since) of the parson apologising for preaching at all: 'I won't keep you for long . . .'; 'I know you're keen to start cooking dinner, but let me just say a few words . . .'

Both the Evangelical and the Tractarian movements stimulated a revival of preaching in the late eighteenth and early nineteenth centuries, but this was mainly confined to towns and cities, with famous preachers like Newman and Smyth attracting huge numbers. In the countryside, and in less distinguished urban parishes, people expected the sermon to be dull and inconsequential, the main interest focusing on how long the parson would continue droning – anything above ten minutes would create an audible stirring of restless bottoms on polished pews. Not surprisingly, many clergy lost confidence in their preaching abilities, regarding the preparation of the Sunday sermon as an unpleasant chore. Alan Bennett's famous spoof of the

Anglican sermon, on the text 'For Esau was a hairy man, but I am a smooth man', was the final straw. Many rural clergy today do little more than cobble together a few random thoughts on the day's lessons and, if questioned on their laxity, they reply that a full-blown sermon to a congregation of five seems absurd.

In the short run the demise of the sermon may not matter. Lay people may with a smile express relief at being spared this weekly dose of boredom, while the clergy feel they have better things to do with their time than to produce five hundred or a thousand words of prose each week, which is then greeted with polite indifference. But in the long term 'the sheep are left hungry', to use a phrase beloved by Puritans. Starved of any regular teaching and guidance, the quality of faith must gradually decline. Moreover, the lack of a good sermon gives people another reason for staying away from church, switching on 'Songs of Praise' instead. Indeed, the very people who once complained that sermons were so dull, will soon be saying: 'If the parson can't be bothered to prepare a sermon, I can't be bothered to attend his services.'

We need in the countryside a fresh style of preaching. The inspiring oration, in which the clergyman stands high in the pulpit declaiming the Gospel, is manifestly inappropriate in a village church. The sermon that can lift two or three hundred hearts in a suburban parish would be merely embarrassing when preached to two elderly ladies and a young family. A more intimate, relaxed way of preaching is required. Happily, we can look in two directions for clues.

There is no audience more demanding than a classroom of small children. Their attention span is short, they are quickly bored, and they easily distract one another. Yet there are thousands of teachers who, at the end of the afternoon when the children are tired and fractious, can gather them together for a story, and hold them spellbound for ten or fifteen minutes. The technique is essentially quite simple, but requires considerable skill and practice. In the first place, the story must contain characters whose moral and emotional qualities are clearly delineated: a 'cruel' giant, a 'gentle' grandmother, a 'sly' fox, a 'jolly' pig. While a novel can contain all sorts of subtleties and innuendoes, a short story spoken out loud must paint a vivid, bright picture in the mind. Secondly, the teacher must express the varying mood and atmosphere of the story in his or her voice. This does not require dramatic shifts in pitch and volume, but rather the natural changes of inflexion which occur in ordinary conversation. The teacher, as it were, 'acts natural'.

The second source of clues is the radio talk. Clergy and lay preachers would do well to listen to those wartime addresses by J. B. Priestley, or any of the hundreds of Letters from America by Alastair Cooke. The audience may run into millions, but for each listener it is an intimate encounter with an old friend, and the listener's attention is held in the palm of the speaker's hand. The techniques of such masters fall into two categories, style and substance. Like the teacher, the radio speaker 'acts natural', reading the script as if sharing in a normal conversation. This in turn requires writing the script in the same short, simple phrases that we use when speaking. The contents of a good radio talk are a blend of pithy observations, sharp illustrations, and clear arguments – always beginning with a statement or image which grabs the attention. The measure of Priestley's and Cooke's success is that they make it sound so easy, yet a fifteen-minute talk may take fifteen hours to prepare. It is truly art concealing art.

Of course, few parsons could emulate those doyens of radio. Furthermore, telling a short story is appropriate only on special occasion, such as Christmas morning or at certain family services. Yet the techniques of teacher and broadcaster apply directly to preaching in village churches. Firstly, a conversational style is vital – which paradoxically requires greater skill than the oratorical style appropriate for large congregations. The parson must learn to write in the same way that he speaks, avoiding great pyramids of sub-clauses, and preferring short, sharp phrases to long circumlocutions. This skill is best honed with the aid of a tape recorder: when a sermon is written, preach it into a microphone, then play it back. Most clergy are horrified at their own pomposity and verbosity, and their hearts go out to their long-suffering parishioners. After two or three revisions the sermon will come right. And once several sermons have been submitted to this gruelling analysis, the knack will have been acquired for life.

A similar double bluff – of learning to sound natural – is required for delivering the sermon. Again a tape recorder can help. Try recording an ordinary spontaneous conversation, and then record a sermon. Most of us when reading out loud sound much flatter, with less variation of pitch, speed and volume, than we do in natural speech. Thus a good sermon can seem dull. There is, of course, a danger into which even some broadcasters fall, of putting so much expression into one's voice that every sentence sounds like an advertisement for a new sports car. Small changes in the pace of delivery, extra emphasis on the key words of each sentence, and slightly raising the voice during more exciting passages, can work wonders. Hard practice, listening to one's errors and correcting them, makes perfect.

For reasons lost in the mists of history the typical sermon is supposed to contain three points. Perhaps the purpose is to assure the congregation, when the parson says 'And thirdly', that the end is nigh. Worse still, prospective clergy are still given the advice which the Puritans followed: 'First say what you are going to say; then say it; and finally say what you've just said.' Broadcasters know by instinct that a good radio talk makes only one point; yet in making that single point repetition is avoided like death. The same should apply to village sermons.

This is not as hard as it sounds. Preparing a short sermon is like cooking a simple dish: there is one essential ingredient. The essential ingredient in this case is a good, vivid illustration, taken from a newspaper, a collection of fables, or even local life. It is worth keeping a file of such illustrations, as almost all regular broadcasters do. Go through the file and pick an illustration which at some point links with the Bible readings. This point of connection becomes the central point of the sermon. Another minor illustration can then be added to the ingredients, plus perhaps one or two apt quotations, for which dictionaries of quotations are a useful stand-by. There is no single formula for mixing these ingredients, but a remarkable proportion of good radio talks actually follow a pattern. They start with an illustration, then draw from the illustration their main point, and conclude with another illustration or quotation which makes that same point in another way. It is not a bad pattern for the short, intimate sermon; but if the ingredients are good enough, almost any way of mixing them will work.

A clergyman some years ago arrived at a group of parishes in Northamptonshire. His predecessor, who had served there for thirty years, had left a letter of advice for the newcomer, at the start of which were the words: 'Preach on any subject you like, except politics and fox-hunting.' The village, needless to say, was the centre of the local hunt. The sensitive parson soon learns the issues where feelings run high, of which party politics is usually near the top of the list, and he and his conscience must decide whether or not to tackle them. But there are two general pieces of advice to follow. Firstly, if the parson can first win the personal trust of the village, he is far more likely to be heard. Indeed, after five years the man in Northamptonshire felt able to express his antipathy to blood sports, and was listened to with respect, whereas if he had spoken out immediately he would have created a barrier of hostility. Secondly, on no account should a sermon ever be used to 'get at' a particular individual or group. In a small community this can inject a dose of resentful anger that spreads through the village, and poisons the entire ministry. Besides, it is cowardly. Country people will take anything from a minister who takes the trouble to understand them, and has the courage to speak his or her mind face to face.

MUST IT ALWAYS BE COMMUNION?

Whenever rural clergy come together to discuss worship, two related issues almost invariably crop up. The first is family services. During the past two or three decades, in town and country alike, churches have experimented with informal styles of worship which appeal to those who find the traditional forms of service too rigid. Some clergy are convinced that family services bring new joy and enthusiasm to Christian life, and are invaluable tools of evangelism, drawing new sheep into the fold. Others regard them as superficial and unsatisfying, pandering to the worse aspects of our television age; and they point out that few people who attend family services progress into full communicant membership of the church.

The second issue is the pattern of Sunday services. For the remote rural clergyman Sunday morning can be a mad dash from one church to another, arriving at each church in time to announce the first hymn, and leaving during the last hymn, the roar of his departing car drowning the final verse. He is too tense and distracted truly to enter the spirit of prayer, and soon comes to regard Sunday worship as a meaningless chore rather than, as it should be, the highlight of the week. Naturally he finds himself yearning for lay people to take some of the services, so that he could enjoy Sunday mornings. But that would mean fewer Communion services, which raises again the question of family services as a substitute.

As is to be expected, these clerical anxieties are echoed in the hearts of many lay people. Some wish to receive Communion each Sunday, and feel let down if only Matins or Evensong or a family service is provided, and, while they may sympathise with the harried parson's predicament, they believe that the church has an obligation to celebrate Communion every Sunday in every parish – and to provide enough clergy for the purpose. Others hanker for the days when Matins and Evensong were the main congregational services, with their stirring canticles and sublime collects; indeed, few could doubt that some of the finest religious poetry ever written – the *Te Deum*, the Collect for Peace – is contained in those services. In some villages the new family services have substantial support.

There is, of course, nothing new about the debate over the form of service; nor is this the first period in history when the countryside has been short of clergy. Although Cranmer intended that the Communion service should remain the centre of Sunday worship, by the late sixteenth century the Puritans were arguing that it should be confined to the major festivals. This was partly to give greater prominence to the sermon as the heart of the service, but it was also because they treated the sacrament with such reverence that they spent many days preparing to receive it, feasting and examining their consciences – and since such rigours could not be endured every week, frequent celebrations of Communion cheapened it. Surprisingly, most High Churchmen accepted the force of this argument; and by the early seventeenth century Communion had become so infrequent in the majority of parishes that Nicholas Ferrar and George Herbert were accused of 'popery' in celebrating the sacrament once a month.

Since Saxon times, when the parochial system was established, the ideal in Britain has been one priest per parish. However, once the Norman conquerors had instituted a separate income for parish clergy, in the form of tithes and rent for glebe land, the way was open for unscrupulous priests to acquire two, three or more parishes, taking the income but neglecting the people. Such pluralism was a running sore throughout the medieval period, but had become an open wound by the eighteenth century. A well-connected clergyman could accumulate huge numbers of parishes, rarely, if ever, visiting them. He either paid an ill-educated curate a tiny stipend to live in each parish, though more probably one of the impoverished priests living in the nearby town rode out on Sunday to take services, receiving one guinea per year for each parish covered. Far from debating the relative merits of Matins or Communion, the parishioners were lucky to hear the words of the service at all, so hastily did the starving cleric gabble them.

In the nineteenth century laws were passed which abolished pluralism, and for a brief golden summer of English parish life almost every village had its resident incumbent. This coincided with a resurgence of religious seriousness, through Evangelical and Tracterian influences. As a result a new pattern of services was instituted throughout the country, in town and village alike, which persisted for almost a century – indeed, anyone over the age of forty today should still be able to remember it. It began with Holy Communion at 8 a.m., at which neither hymns were sung nor a sermon preached. At 11 a.m. there was High

Matins, the main service of the day: a robed choir led the singing, which included psalms, canticles and hymns, as well as responses during the prayers; and the parson preached a sermon usually lasting about ten minutes. This was followed immediately afterwards at 12.15 by a short Communion service, for which a small minority stayed behind: it started at the offertory, and lasted only around twenty minutes. The day finished with Evensong, usually at eight o'clock, when again hymns were sung and the parson, if he were so inclined, was allowed to preach at greater length.

Many older people recall this pattern with nostalgia, but in the 1950s and 1960s three factors combined to destroy it. Firstly, the 'Parish and People' movement won widespread support among clergy of all descriptions, as well as among many influential lay people, in its campaign to promote the 'Parish Communion' as the main Sunday service. It is strange in retrospect that the Tractarians a century earlier, who were seeking to reintroduce ancient Catholic practices, had been content to make Matins the central service. But in this century Evangelicals and High Churchmen alike were convinced by the argument that Jesus himself intended his followers to receive the sacrament each week. Secondly, congregations at Evensong slumped, persuading many clergy to drop it. The popularity of *The Forsyte Saga* is usually blamed, but one suspects 'Songs of Praise' should bear some responsibility!

The third factor, which has proved most important in the countryside, has been the dearth of clergy. Since the First World War pluralism has reappeared with a vengeance, due not to greed, but to lack of money and manpower. Thus a country parson, with four, six or eight parishes under his wing, is hard-pressed to reach all his churches once a fortnight, let alone take three services in each church every Sunday. To add insult to injury, the new emphasis on Parish Communion leaves the typical country clergyman with a perpetual sense of spiritual failure. His training at theological college has convinced him that his people should receive the sacrament each week; and if, like his Victorian predecessor, he had a single parish he could institute such a policy. But under present circumstances he must give his congregation second best – or so he feels.

To escape from this trap of decline and failure, we must stand back and question the wisdom of our time. The Parish Communion is merely the current fashion, just as High Matins was the fashion of the Victorian age, and, while it is now taken for granted by clergy and laity alike in our towns and cities, there remains deep-seated resistance in the countryside. The main objection is that it is 'exclusive': only those who are committed members of the church, and have been confirmed, can participate, while the remainder of the village feel pushed out. Beneath this anxiety is the question of who really belongs to the church, as we explored earlier. In an urban parish it is now appropriate to have a clear membership list, comprising only a tiny fraction of the local population, and these people constitute the Anglican family in that place. But in a village almost everyone still regards that ancient building with the spire as 'our church', and the land around it as 'our churchyard', and many who would not dream of coming to church regularly want to be able to attend services from time to time – after a bereavement, before a wedding, or simply when the mood takes them.

It is at least open to argument as to whether Jesus really did intend us to receive the sacrament every week, as distinct from every day, every month or every year. Among those early Anglicans who took the sacrament extremely seriously, Nicholas Ferrar and George Herbert regarded monthly Communion as optimal: it was neither too frequent to cheapen it, nor too rare to deprive the soul of its blessing. While acknowledging that other opinions and preferences are equally valid, it would be a great relief to most rural clergy, and a matter of joy to many of the rural laity, if the wisdom of Ferrar and Herbert again held sway in the countryside. A parson with eight parishes could without strain celebrate Communion on one Sunday morning per month in each church; and a parson with as many as twelve parishes could also achieve a monthly cycle, if some of his churches were willing to receive the sacrament in the afternoon or evening. It is worth noting that a monthly visit from the priest is a great deal better than many parts of the Anglican Communion enjoy: in Uganda, for example, one clergyman covers sixteen or twenty rural parishes, with only a bicycle to carry him between them.

The other services in the month would thus be non-Eucharistic which, in the case of large groups of parishes, would be taken by unpaid clergy, by readers, or even by churchwardens. The first question is whether every church should strive to have a service every Sunday, or whether perhaps once a fortnight is sufficient. Ferrar and Herbert certainly believed that Christians should attend public worship each Sunday, and few today would dissent from that principle. Yet when surveys are taken in even the most flourishing suburban church, it turns out that people on average attend worship only two or three times each month; on the other Sundays they are visiting relatives, going for a trip in the country or simply lying in bed. Happily in rural churches, which for many years have had services only once a fortnight, people get into the habit of going out or oversleeping on the Sundays when there is no service. In practice, therefore, they attend worship almost as frequently as their suburban counterparts. The consequence is that these churches tend to have better congregations than those which struggle to maintain a weekly service.

The conclusion, then, is that if there are sufficient clergy and lay readers to conduct services every week in every church, then as a matter of principle this pattern should be continued. But if this puts undue strain on those leading worship, forcing them to rush from one church to another, then a fortnightly service is better. Indeed, as most clergy would affirm, those few relaxed minutes after a service spent chatting to parishioners can be invaluable, both in cementing friendships with the church-goers themselves, and in providing pastoral information about others in the village.

Now comes the knotty problem of the form of non-Eucharistic service: traditional Matins or Evensong, versus the modern family service. The short answer is to discover which works best in each particular village. If the parish contains lots of young children, the family service is the ideal vehicle for getting them – and their parents – into church. Bright, popular hymns can be sung; children with musical abilities can be persuaded to play instruments, and others can be organised to put on little plays to illustrate the Bible readings; and the person preaching can tell stories, or use simple visual aids, to hold the children's attention. Such services do, of course, require tremendous preparation but, as a means of reaching out to the village as a whole, they are ideal. Moreover, even if the parents never become communicants, at least they are imbibing the church message, and their children are being led towards adult faith.

There are, however, two snags. The first is that some regular church-goers loathe them, while the second is that they only work with a dozen or more children in attendance, which many smaller villages cannot muster. In such circumstances straightforward Matins or Evensong, according to the Book of Common Prayer, may be the answer. However, many rural parishes are hitting on a happy compromise, in which the traditional services are adapted to suit every taste and age. The versicles and responses are preserved, as they provide an enjoyable spiritual dialogue which is well suited to small congregations, and which children can enjoy; so also are the collects and general confession, whose sublime phrases can germinate in even the youngest mind, to give great spiritual sustenance in adult life. But the traditional psalms and canticles can be replaced by more melodic versions, such as 'Tell out my soul' for the *Magnificat*, and even one of the more popular metrical psalms such as 'The Lord's my Shepherd' in place of the psalm of the day. There can be a single Bible reading, with occasionally a 'tableau' or play where the second lesson comes, and the sermon can be accessible to children – as, indeed, any good sermon should be.

Once the clergyman stops rushing, and once he and his people discover the advantages of small congregations, then worship in the countryside is second to none. Anyone who has attended Evensong in an ancient village church in late spring, and come out as the sun was setting behind the spire, has come as near to heaven as this mortal life allows.

3

MINISTRY

WHAT SHOULD THE PARSON BE UP TO?

The typical country parson today feels overburdened. As he looks out of his vicarage window across the field, to distant spires on the horizon, he is filled with anxiety and even dread. To a friend standing beside him, the view is tranquil and enchanting, but to the clergyman each spire represents another community under his spiritual care, with its own particular needs and problems. He wistfully thinks of the days a century ago when each parson had a single parish, leaving him time to write scholarly tomes, to study the local fauna and flora, and simply to relax. Now even his few leisured moments are likely to be interrupted by a phone call about next months' fete in one of his parishes, or next Sunday's christening in another.

When an attempt is made to analyse the country parson's time, however, it turns out that many actually do very little. A large number of separate parishes can turn Sunday mornings into a mad dash from one to another, and extra parishes mean additional Parochial Church Council meetings. Yet even as many as twelve parishes, which is exceptionally high, implies only forty-eight PCC meetings each year – slightly less than one a week. Most urban clergy, by contrast, expect to have twice as many church meetings, when all the various sub-committees of a large parish are taken into account. When it comes to baptisms, weddings and funerals, these multiply as a proportion of the population, not the number of parishes. So a rural clergyman with, say, two thousand people scattered over six villages, may have between ten and twenty weddings and baptisms a year, and twice as many funerals; while his urban colleague, with ten thousand people concentrated in a single parish, has four or five times as many.

The reason for this paradox is that the country parson is often extremely unclear as to what he should be up to between Monday and Saturday – and there are few things more stressful than uncertainty. Indeed, the paucity of meetings, and of baptisms, weddings and funerals, is to some degree the source of the problem. While the urban clergyman's diary is so full that he has no time to reflect on the value of what he is doing, the diary of the country parson is filled with blank spaces in which to fret and worry. Worse still, there are no objectives to pursue, no parochial achievements to chalk up. While urban ministers can busy themselves with all manner of imaginative projects, from introducing new styles of worship on Sunday morning, to starting up playschools for the young and clubs for the elderly, the experienced rural clergyman has long since learned that such projects generally turn to dust in the countryside: the worshippers resist novelty, and families and old people in small communities can come together informally without the parson's help. As for visiting, there is a limit to the number of times even the sick and the housebound want to see the vicar. Some rural clergy fill their days by sitting on diocesan committees and attending all manner of courses and discussion groups, but this only suppresses the nagging doubts.

At the heart of the issue is our understanding of the ordained ministry. Over the past century and a half our view of the clergyman's role has been fashioned by the city and the suburb. We remember those indomitable priests of the Victorian age, trained in the strict disciplines of the Tractarian movement, who took the slums of London and Manchester by storm: in church on Sunday clouds of incense wafted round dazzling vestments and altars, to the delight of hungry families in rags; and during the week the priest laboured hard to fill their stomachs and clothe their bodies. We remember, too, those passionate Evangelical preachers of the industrial towns, who on the sabbath held thousands of illiterate men and women spellbound for hours on end by their fiery oratory, and who on every evening of the week organised bible studies and prayer meetings by the score.

In the more comfortable and complacent atmosphere of the present age such magisterial characters are rare, yet urban ministers and vicars, consciously or not, may still model themselves on their example. On Sunday services are conducted that are filled with action and colour, so that even a congregation jaded by the tricks of television is kept on the edge of the pews. At the end of each service an array of meetings are announced for the coming week: cubs, brownies, scouts, guides, youth club, young wives' group, bible study, over sixties club, prayer meeting – and during Lent a multiplicity of house groups. The minister stands at the centre of this bustle, as both master of ceremonies and managing director, encouraging and instructing those who have an active role to play in the worship, chairing many of the committees which run the different aspects of parish life, as well as chairing the church's board of directors, the PCC; while across his or her desk pass all the letters and documents essential to such a flourishing enterprise.

Not every urban and suburban parish conforms to this image of success; indeed, there are many, especially in the inner cities, which struggle to survive. But it is the mark to which many vicars aim. Thus, quite naturally, when a clergyman moves from town to countryside, he aims at the same mark – and judges his own ministry by whether he hits it. Small wonder that so many rural parsons feel themselves to be failures. Initially the parishioners show polite interest in his ideas, and may even attend meetings and house groups which he organises. But he soon discovers that such gatherings will only survive if he continues to head them, and exerts unflagging moral pressure on people to keep coming. In desperation he may invite some famous figure to come and speak one evening at the vicarage; and then finds himself profusely apologising that only three people have turned up – 'There must be something else on in the village,' he hears himself saying, covered in blushes. He may, on arrival at his new cure, have had some clear objectives; but after a year or two his enthusiasm and energy have been drained, and he feels exhausted.

Fortunately, however, a growing number of rural clergy are discovering a quite different model of ministry. They are breaking free from the chains of the urban model, and leaping back in history to the centuries prior to industrialisation. Here they find that the village priest was indeed the 'parson' – the person who embodied the moral and spiritual values of the community. It was not what he did that counted, but what he was. The good parson was one whose life was holy and blameless, and who loved his people, sharing their joys and their sorrows. His sermons were not masterpieces of oratory, but were filled with homely metaphors and illustrations that he had gleaned from village life. His services were never exciting or entertaining, but their quiet dignity offered peace and serenity to troubled hearts. When he was neither praying nor visiting his people, he was digging his garden or studying works of Christian scholarship. He had no desire to achieve anything in his parish, but simply to be 'God's person' in that place.

The most masterly and beautiful exposition of this style of ministry is George Herbert's *A Priest to the Temple, or the Country Parson*, written in the early 1630s. He recognised that in his day, as in ours, rural ministry is 'somewhat despised' by the world, and the country parson 'held in contempt'. Yet he speaks of the parson as Christ's 'vice-regent' who must live by the very highest moral standards – indeed, the quality of his life is his most eloquent sermon. During the week his ministry consists of prayer, in which he confides in God the needs of his flock, person by person, and visiting, in which he befriends each person and responds to their needs, spiritual and material. In the most enchanting passage Herbert describes the herbs which the parson should grow in his garden – hyssop, valerian, elder, camomile, comfrey, St John's wort – to provide salves, poultices and medicines for the sick. On Sundays, in addition to leading worship, he spends the day 'reconciling neighbours that are at variance, or in exhortation to some of his flock by themselves, who his sermons cannot, or do not reach.'

Faced with Herbert's 'mark to aim at', the modern clergyman finds himself reacting in two opposite ways. In terms of achievement, Herbert seems to be aiming too low: his ministry is passive, representing God without visibly changing and improving the church and the village; and some might even accuse him (as his contemporaries did) of escapism, retreating from the real challenges of the world into some nostalgic rural fantasy. In terms of morality, however, modern clergy would find his mark too high: he wants the parson to be a veritable saint, without fault or flaw. Yet the sole passage of Scripture which outlines the qualities required in a church leader, 1 Timothy 3: 1–7, gives surprising credence to Herbert's view. There is no mention here of talents and gifts, such as good oratory, managerial abilities, social skills – the kinds of things which modern selection conferences look for in putative clergy. On the contrary, with the exception of the ability to teach, the list consists entirely of moral and spiritual virtues: he must be sober, dignified, peaceful, gentle, a faithful husband, devoid of all greed, hospitable, generous, prayerful, mature in faith – in short, holy.

Of course, no one who is remotely holy imagines himself to be so; so, like Herbert himself, no one who is suitable to be such a parson would regard himself as such. But the point is that the country parson, in Herbert's model, is someone who wants above all things to *become* holy, who puts moral and spiritual virtue above all other objectives and values. If we look round at the rural clergy today it is indeed those who are holy, even saintly, whose ministries seem to flourish. In a small community the parishioners soon get to know their parson as he truly is; he cannot for long put up a front. They are willing to forgive any practical flaws and lack of skills – dull preaching, shyness, inefficiency – if he is loving and generous, and is a shining example to them and their children. They do not want him propping up the bar every night at the village pub (although an occasional visit is welcome) nor do they want him trying to be one of the lads, swapping rude jokes. Rather they want to be assured that he is a loving and considerate husband and father, and that he genuinely cares about every member of his parishes. For all his limitations and failures in practical affairs, such a man genuinely does represent God to his people, and for that he is loved and cherished by them.

Some clergy, sensing these moral expectations, feel themselves caught in a trap. In all humility they know they cannot meet such exacting standards; and yet, out of love for their people, they do not want to disillusion them by revealing their feet of clay. So they distance themselves, frightened to form real friendships within their parishes in which people come to know them as they really are. They may even, despite their better instincts, create a mask for themselves, saying and doing in public what they imagine people want, while suppressing their genuine personality. As a result they feel lonely and isolated, which is a horribly common hazard of rural ministry. Not surprisingly, many come to feel quite bitter that, while living within a close-knit community, they alone feel excluded from its warmth by being put on a moral pedestal.

The simple answer for a parson in such a plight is to go and talk about it to some of the lay people in his congregations. They will understand his position, because to some degree the village as a whole places similar expectations on their shoulders as regular worshippers; in a quite palpable sense, the worshipping congregation as an entity, as well as the parson on his own, represents God within the village. But they will reassure him that there is no need for pretence or for isolation. They ask only of him that he sincerely wishes to follow the Christian way in every aspect of his life; his stumbles on that path cause no upset or disillusionment, but enable them to identify more closely with him, and so respond more easily to his moral leadership. Once the parson understands this, he is free to make normal, human friendships with his parishioners.

George Herbert, during the three short years in which he served as a country parson, was never overworked, nor did he feel any guilt about the hours spent listening to music, writing poetry, and tending his garden. Similarly today, if country parsons sought to emulate Herbert's style of ministry, the stress which so many feel would melt away. Their work consists of leading worship on Sunday, of visiting and encouraging their people during the week, and of praying for their people every day; if the population in their care is sufficiently small that this takes only three or four days, they are free, like Herbert, to pursue other interests – until, of course the bishop finds out, and gives them more parishes!

HOW CAN ONE PARSON COPE WITH NUMEROUS VILLAGES?

In 1981 a clergyman arrived in Northamptonshire to be vicar of four small rural parishes. His vicarage was in the largest village, which until his arrival had been on its own with a parson to itself. The other three villages had for the previous seventy years been in a group sharing a parson. The new clergyman thus found himself ministering to two villages which had not had a resident clergyman since the First World War; one village which had just lost its resident clergyman, so that an estate agent's board hung outside the old vicarage; and one village which had always had a resident clergyman, but was now forced to share his time with the others.

He expected that his ministry would be easiest and most fruitful in the parish where he lived; after all, they seemingly had come out best in the new arrangement, retaining a parson and his family within the community. He also assumed that the parishes which had lost their parson three generations ago would be virtually moribund, having lacked clerical leadership for so long. To his amazement the opposite was the case. The parishes without a parson had long since learned to run the church themselves, organising their own fund-raising activities, looking after the church fabric, visiting the sick and elderly – and even, when necessary, conducting worship with one of the churchwardens reading the service. They were grateful and appreciative of everything that the new clergyman did, and thanked him for breathing new life into their services; but they did not depend on him to manage their affairs, and so did not grumble or complain at his limitations. The parish where he lived, by contrast, expected him to do everything, from editing the parish magazine to ensuring that the church was kept clean, because that was what their vicar had always done, and whenever anything went wrong, however trivial, complaints landed at his doorstep. Most astonishing of all, the congregations were actually larger in the two smallest parishes.

Many rural clergy could tell a different story: the congregations who ceased to have a vicar long ago have become demoralised, and deeply resent the cavalier way they feel the diocese have treated them, while the parish where the vicar lives flourishes. But when one looks beneath the surface, the picture is almost always the same. A rural church blossoms to the extent to which the congregation as a whole manages itself, with the vicar making his particular contribution; while the church which looks to the vicar to run everything gradually wilts.

We should not, of course, be surprised: it is what the Bible leads us to expect. In the vibrant churches which Paul founded, everyone was encouraged to exercise a ministry – as a prophet, teacher, healer, administrator – and thus become an active 'organ' in the body of Christ. Even more pertinent for our present discussion is the evolution of the church in Jerusalem as described in the Acts of the Apostles. At first the apostles did everything, from preaching and leading worship to managing the finances, but as the church grew it became painfully obvious that even those great figures, commissioned by Jesus himself, were incompetent in practical matters, and so people began to grumble and complain. The matter came to a head over the distribution of food to the elderly widows, where some were actually going hungry. Yet, far from clinging to power, the apostles, as soon as they realised the problem, proposed that seven deacons be appointed to manage all financial and practical affairs, leaving them free for preaching and prayer.

Thus at a very early stage in the church's history a twofold structure of leadership was established, roughly corresponding to the spiritual and material aspects of the community's life. This structure did not, however, remain rigid or static; almost as soon as Stephen and Philip have been appointed as managers, we see them preaching and evangelising. People were thus not to be confined by the particular task assigned to them, but were free to exercise all their gifts. The apostles themselves saw their ministry as mobile, travelling from place to place spreading the good news; indeed, the word 'apostle' means 'ambassador', implying a peripatetic ministry. Thus they appointed local preachers and pastors to care permanently for each congregation.

The denomination within Britain that has most clearly conformed to this Jerusalem model of ministry is the Methodist Church. John Wesley saw himself as an apostle, riding tens of thousands of miles across the country to preach the gospel, and very soon he appointed local preachers to continue his ministry in each place where a Methodist group formed. Once these groups began to accumulate funds of their own, and at a later stage to build chapels of their own, stewards were appointed to manage these assets. Class leaders were also chosen, each with a small group to look after, caring for their personal needs and guiding them in their spiritual progress. To a remarkable extent this original structure has survived, and enables large numbers of people to exercise an active and responsible ministry. The apostles of Wesley's day have become the ordained ministers, paid by the congregations they serve, in order to work full time for the church. Inevitably, in some places these ministers have accumulated too much power and responsibility for themselves, hence stifling the gifts of others, but happily a combination of financial poverty and shortage of vocations has kept the number of ministers low, so congregations have been forced to rely on themselves. Moreover, the stewards appoint the ministers, and so act as a permanent check on clerical power.

In theory the Church of England has a similar structure – indeed, Wesley was inspired not only by the Bible, but by Anglicanism at its best. In law the churchwardens have much the same powers as the Methodist stewards: they are responsible for the material assets of the church, including the building. They are also required to exercise discipline within the church, throwing out anyone who misbehaves during worship (which is why a churchwarden carries a staff as the sign of his office). Thus the division of function between churchwarden and vicar should be much like that between deacon and apostle in the Jerusalem church. To emphasise the independent authority of the churchwarden within the parish, he is, according to canon law, directly answerable to the bishop, as the vicar himself is, so within their respective spheres churchwardens and vicar should stand as equals.

The truth is that for the past two or three centuries this dual form of leadership has in practice become a hierarchy, with the vicar at the top, and the churchwardens as his assistants. To resist this tendency, many parishes (quite illegally) used to have a 'vicar's warden', chosen by the clergyman, and a 'people's warden', elected by the congregation, so that at least one of the churchwardens had an independent voice. Fortunately, this practice has almost entirely lapsed, so that all churchwardens are now formally elected at the parish annual general meeting. Yet the fact that the parson is working full time for the church, while the churchwardens are volunteers with only a few hours spare each week to devote to their task, means that the parson tends to manage the church's affairs, as well as preach and pray. Few churchwardens have the time or the will to seize power back for themselves.

In the countryside, however, the new pluralism is gradually shifting the balance. A clergyman with four or six small parishes can probably still remain the boss of all of them. Indeed, his parishioners, including the churchwardens, will expect this of him, since he manifestly has sufficient time to do so – to meet builders and architects about the church fabric, to organise the fund-raising appeals, and so on. But once the number of parishes under a single full-time clergyman rises to eight or even ten, the hierarchical model crumbles. He simply has neither the energy nor the hours in the day to be both apostle and deacon. Like the members of the Jerusalem church, the parishioners' first reaction is usually to grumble at the vicar's inefficiency: 'Why isn't the fête properly organised?' they ask accusingly; 'Why has the vicar still not arranged glaziers to repair the church window?' they add, looking up at the glass shattered three months earlier by stray shot. Slowly it dawns that the vicar, without risking a nervous breakdown, simply cannot run their fête or repair their windows. If these things are to be done, they must do them themselves.

That moment of truth is the start of a new reformation, which should be far deeper in its effects in the countryside than the first reformation was. The parson of many parishes has no choice but to confine himself to being an apostle and, like the first apostles in Jerusalem, he must politely and humbly ask his people to choose from among themselves deacons who can run their affairs, in the form of churchwardens and PCC members. At first they may be reluctant, greatly overestimating both the time and the expertise needed to manage a church. The parson can, however, assure them that, as far as management is con-

'cerned, they are probably more skilled than he is, since his training at college was confined to spiritual and theological matters; and if they spread the load between them it should not be unduly time-consuming.

Clergy who have been forced to enact this reformation are almost invariably delighted with the results. In fact, far from resenting the number of parishes in their cure, they come to regard it as a blessing. They can now concentrate on the ministry to which God has called them, and for which they devoted three or four years of training: leading worship, and caring for the spiritual needs of their people. They can devote ample time to serious reading and to preparing their sermons, free from the unrelenting practical demands that hitherto sapped their energy. They can spend two, three or four afternoons each week visiting their people, simply to befriend them – rather than to beg money, or pressurise them into helping at the fête or coffee evening. When the fête and coffee evening occur, they can chat to people, rather than rush round seeing that the stalls are properly organised. As the apostles in Jerusalem found, they are liberated to be themselves.

As the number of rural clergy has declined over the past seventy years, many people have accused the Church of England of 'retreating from the countryside'. They fear that without abundant clergy the church itself will disappear, and they point to the Methodists, and other Nonconformist denominations, where the laity, deprived of paid ministers, have proved unable to cope. Such anxieties are surely misplaced. The decline of Nonconformity has far deeper roots; and, besides, the withdrawal of the paid ministry was the consequence, not the cause, of this decline, for the tiny congregations could no longer afford their stipends. More fundamentally, the current weakness of so many rural parishes is precisely because for too long the church has been identified with its clergy, thereby stifling the abundant spiritual and practical gifts of its members. One shudders to think what St Paul would make of the phrase, 'I've decided to go into the church' (meaning 'I've decided to be ordained'). Paul's passionate belief in the ministry of all believers applies supremely to the rural congregation.

The parson, therefore, can cope quite happily with a large number of parishes if he insists on others sharing the task, and the best way to ensure that people respond is not by words, but by necessity. It is precisely because he has so many parishes that the people are compelled to take responsibility.

HOW CAN MINISTRY BE SHARED?

As soon as a vicar announces that he will be leaving in three or six months' time, the churchwardens and members of the PCC swing into action. Arrangements are made for worship after his departure, inviting clergy and readers from elsewhere for some services, and filling the gaps with the churchwardens leading Matins or Evensong. The organisation of parish events, such as the harvest supper, is taken over by a small group convened for the purpose, and the churchwardens take from the vicar the file containing all the correspondence with the church architect and building contractors. Thus when the vicar finally bids farewell and the interregnum begins, the organisation of the church continues to purr smoothly. Six months, a year or even longer may elapse while a replacement is sought, during which everyone pulls together, willingly undertaking whatever the churchwardens ask; and for years after the new vicar has arrived, the interregnum is remembered with nostalgia as a golden moment in the church's history.

Yet this story is not relayed to the bishop and archdeacon when they visit the PCC during the interregnum. Almost every parish begs to have as large a share of a vicar as the diocese will permit, and they bitterly resist any proposal to put the parish in a larger group. They tell the bishop and archdeacon that, without a large chunk of a vicar's time to run their affairs, their Christian community will become demoralised and steadily die. The bishop and archdeacon are naturally impressed by these arguments; after all, they are clergymen themselves, and are gratified to hear of the enormous importance which the laity attach to the clergy. So, although at times they may be compelled to put parishes into larger groups, they enact such measures with great reluctance.

There is a parallel schizophrenia in the attitude of the clergy themselves. Over recent decades umpteen conferences have been convened at which rural parsons have discussed lay ministry; to a man they are in favour of lay people becoming more active in the spiritual ministry of the church. They like the idea of lay people helping to conduct services, leading house groups, and visiting the sick and the elderly. They support the notion of training lay people in these various pastoral tasks, and for the most part they are happy in principle with particular lay people being authorised by the bishop as 'elders' or 'pastoral assistants'. Like virtue itself, lay ministry is universally applauded by the rural clergy.

However, as many lay people have found to their cost, the story can be quite different in practice. Many rural clergy quite understandably feel threatened by the more capable and well-educated laity taking over some of their traditional roles. The prospect of a broadcaster or barrister who lives in the village training as a reader, and then preaching lively and stimulating sermons, can make a rural parson shudder with fear; he, after all, is being paid to preach his rather lack-lustre sermons. The thought of house groups erupting in every village, under the skilled leaderships of local teachers, lecturers and the like, can seem to strike at the heart of the parson's authority; he imagines these groups dictating to him how the worship and management of the parishes should be conducted. Friendly housewives spending a few hours visiting the sick seem less threatening; but here too, if he is somewhat shy and diffident himself, he cannot help wondering if people will prefer their homely chat to his stilted conversation. The clergyman knows that he should not feel these anxieties, and may even regard them as sinful; but he is as vulnerable and insecure as the rest of the human race.

The sad consequence of this ambivalence is that progress towards a truly shared ministry has been slow and patchy. It is not uncommon for, say, a deanery to put on a lay training course during which people attend a study group for one evening a week over a year, only to discover at the end that their vicars have no substantial role for them to play. Some rural dioceses, such as Edmundsbury and Ely, have a system of lay pastorship, in which a PCC, in collaboration with the vicar, can nominate people as 'elders', who are then authorised by the bishop at a special service. Yet these elders find all too frequently that their vicar simply does not know what to do with them, offering neither guidance nor encouragement. Paradoxically, it is often those clergy who seem most in need of help that are least willing to receive it: their lack of self-confidence makes them fearful of any intrusion. Fortunately, there are some groups of parishes where lay ministry thrives, to the delight of the incumbent, but these remain the exception.

The key to shared ministry is division of labour: the clergy, and the various lay ministers, should have clearly defined tasks, which they are free to tackle in their own way, without fear of trivial interference. The parson should see himself, and be seen by others, as the conductor of the spiritual orchestra. He should seek to discern the various spiritual gifts among his people, and encourage them to exercise those gifts. Where appropriate, he should ensure that they receive the training they need, and thereafter, month by month, year by year, he should remain in close touch, helping them to think through for themselves how to meet the various challenges and problems confronting them. The aim should be that in every parish there is a warm Christian community, whose members are both ministering to each other, and ministering to the village as a whole.

Advocates of such a shared ministry are often eager to propose radical schemes to rejig the church's structure. Lay eldership has been one such scheme; others include 'ministerial teams', consisting of both clergy and laity, covering a whole deanery (and keeping in touch by mobile phones in their cars!). Country people treat these ideas with caution, knowing that they cause a great deal of disruption while achieving very little, and are then abandoned after five fiery years. They also suspect that they are a diocesan ruse to deprive them of their vicar, and undermine the time-honoured ministry of the church. In one respect that cautious reaction is quite justified: in an institution with such deep and ancient roots as the Church of England, whose members are lovingly attached to its traditions, radical experiments are at best ineffective, at worst disastrous. In another respect, however, stubborn resistance is self-defeating. The time-honoured ministry has already been undermined by clergy shortages, and can only be restored and maintained by incorporating lay people. Shared ministry should thus be seen not as a radical step, but as a conservative one, aimed at upholding the best pastoral traditions of the Church of England.

The existing structure of the Church of England is, however, perfectly adequate; we simply need to make full use of it. We have already seen how the churchwardens should be given the importance that their ancient office deserves: they, not the vicar, should manage the church's material affairs, and the Parochial Church Council exists to help and guide them. By law the parson should act as chairman of the PCC. This can work perfectly well so long as he treats the role as pastoral, rather than administrative. At the meetings he should encourage people to speak their minds, ensuring that the less articulate express their views, and then steer the meeting towards a common mind; but the secretary and the churchwardens should set the agenda, and implement the decisions. Some excellent parsons, however, make rotten chairmen; besides, if the parson has a large number of parishes, it may be unfair to expect him to attend every PCC, and parishes should therefore appoint a good vice-chairman to take his place when necessary.

When it comes to the pastoral ministry, the Church of England can ordain both voluntary (non-stipendiary) clergy and readers to conduct worship and give spiritual succour. The problem is that we do not have nearly enough such people. In many people's eyes the office of reader seems rather drab and dull, and people who are eminently suitable are reluctant to consider it. This, in part at least, is because it involves quite a long and rigorous training; yet at the end the reader's role depends almost entirely on the whim of the parson. A similar snag attaches to the voluntary clergy. In addition, many lay people with the right gifts regard themselves, in honest humility, as unworthy. A further stumbling-block is also sometimes mentioned: that priests, deacons and, to a lesser degree, readers should in some respect be 'set apart', with the result that people feel diffident in assuming these roles in communities where they have lived as ordinary laity for many years.

All these objections should be swept aside. In his or her own village a reader or voluntary priest or deacon should, to a great extent, assume the role of parson. This does not mean usurping the paid parson, but rather working with and under him, as the clergy work with and under the bishop. In other words, a large group of parishes should function like a mini-diocese, with the paid clergyman as 'bishop', and a voluntary minister in as many individual villages as possible. The voluntary minister could perhaps chair the PCC (in practice, if not in law), visit the sick and elderly, administer Communion where appropriate, and be the first point of contact concerning baptisms and weddings. He or she would also arrange the Sunday services, in co-operation with the paid parson. Funeral arrangements, however, would probably need to remain in the parson's hands, as these usually have to be carried out during working hours, but the voluntary minister should certainly be in close touch with the parson over many other areas.

The voluntary minister would thus have a status and role that was to a great extent independent of the paid clergyman. Equally, he or she would not threaten the paid clergyman, but rather enhance his position. There could not, of course, be rigid demarcation between paid and voluntary ministers. The voluntary minister, who has a demanding job during the day, could not be expected to give more than one or two evenings a week to his ministry, plus one service on Sunday. This is generally adequate in most small villages, but there will be times when greater effort is needed, and then the paid parson must step into the breach. If the parson and the voluntary minister can meet once a month, in an atmosphere of mutual trust, any minor tensions should be quickly eased. As for the anxiety that the clergyman or reader should be 'set apart', this, as we discussed earlier, is based on a false understanding of ministry. When a local parson is ordained, his ministry is actually enriched by people's knowledge of his faults and flaws. It is his sincere desire to be holy, not his achievement of holiness, which qualifies him as a minister, and his manifest faults enable others to identify more easily with his efforts to overcome them!

If such a pattern is to be enacted in the countryside, the first priority is to recruit people to the voluntary ministry. There is in Anglican circles an unfortunate and misguided assumption that individuals should only be ordained if they first experience an inner calling, and then offer themselves for selection. This was not, of course, how Peter, James, John and the rest became apostles; Jesus invited them and, without any prior sense of vocation, they accepted. Equally today it should be the church, as the body of Christ, which discerns people's gifts, and invites them to exercise those gifts. Thus in a rural parish both the paid parson and the laity should look within their community for someone, or even two or three people, who may be suitable as voluntary ministers, and then ask them to serve. They would, of course, need to be approved by the bishop and his selectors, yet even here the underlying purpose would be to ratify the local church's judgement, rather than put an individual to the test. There are abundant stories from the early centuries of the church of men being dragged to the altar to be ordained, loudly protesting their unworthiness. Anglicans usually conduct themselves more decorously nowadays, but the parson and the lay people of a parish should nevertheless use all their persuasive powers on any suitable candidate.

At first sight it may seem rather fanciful to envisage a large group of rural parishes, with one paid clergyman, and a number of voluntary clergy and readers in each village, yet this is precisely how the Anglican Church is organised in most of the rest of the world. In most African countries, for example, the parson has sixteen or twenty churches in his cure; and since he travels on foot or by bicycle, he visits only one or two each Sunday. He in turn, with the help of the laity, finds one or two people in each village to train as readers, who then lead worship in the intervening weeks. Far from being a recipe for a weak, insipid spiritual life, the African church is vibrant, and growing by leaps and bounds. Within each village the close pastoral care, in which Anglicanism in England used to pride itself, is given in abundant measure: the local readers, born and bred in the villages where they serve, prove the most loving shepherds of their people.

CAN LAY PEOPLE BE PASTORS?

Ten years ago a new vicar arrived at a group of four parishes in Cambridgeshire. On his first Sunday his heart fell when he saw how small the congregations were: even the largest village could muster only six people in church. Two of the parishes boasted branches of the Mothers' Union, and he assumed that their membership would be even smaller. But when he attended their meetings, he was amazed to find them packed out: one branch had twenty ladies, crammed into the front parlour of a farmhouse, while the other had sixteen, sitting on canvas chairs in the village hall.

His first reaction was to feel hurt, that so many people turned out to Mothers' Union gatherings while so few found their way to his services in church; surely, he felt, it should be the other way round. Then be began to speculate on the reasons. Perhaps the talks at the Mothers' Union were more exciting than his sermons; but after enduring three or four speakers of mind-numbing dullness, his self-confidence was restored. Perhaps people could not bear the damp coldness of church; yet the village hall used by one branch was almost as bad. Perhaps the elaborate preparations for Sunday lunch left no time for worship; but for working women, coming out on a mid-week evening was quite a rush. Finally he plucked up courage to ask some of the members why they were so loyal to the Mothers' Union. 'I like to come because all my friends come,' replied one. 'Doris, the enrolling member, gives us such a warm welcome,' said another. 'It feels like a real community,' answered a third. 'We look after each other, especially when anyone is sick,' said a fourth. In short, they came to the meetings not for the speaker, but for each other; the congregation in church lacked that sense of solidarity.

Sadly there is often tension between the vicar and any lay organisations in his parishes, of which the Mothers' Union is the most common. He may see them as a substitute church, draining away the energy and commitment that should be given to the parish as a whole. Worse still, they may appear as a bastion of power, determined to resist any innovations within the parish which he may propose. They in turn often feel slighted by the parson, complaining that he does not give them the attention and support which they deserve. To its credit the Mothers' Union from its outset anticipated this danger, and sought to integrate itself within the parochial structure: the vicar appoints the enrolling member, who leads the branch, and he even has power to close the branch down. Despite this authority, however, too many vicars regard their branch with polite distrust.

Yet if such lay organisations are open and outward-looking, and if their members are truly loyal to the parish church, they can be a priceless complement to the parson's own ministry. They are our nearest modern equivalent to the groups of 'widows' described in the Acts of the Apostles and the First Epistle to Timothy, who looked after the sick, fed the hungry, and nurtured new converts. Similarly, a good Mothers' Union branch visits and supports not only its own sick members, but anyone in the parish who is ill: they send a card and a bunch of flowers, ensure that one or two members pay a visit, and offer to do the shopping or any other practical jobs that are needed. They also keep an eye on any newcomers to the village, welcoming them and ensuring that they make friends.

The Mothers' Union and other such bodies are, of course, formal organisations and, from what we can gather, the groups of widows in the early church were formalised to the extent of having rules of membership – only women of unquestioned virtue who had no intention of remarrying were acceptable. If one looks closely, however, there is in most parishes an informal band of women and men who, without asking for any recognition or gratitude, respond to people's needs. They are the ones who, when an elderly person can no longer cook, will bring meals; who, when someone dies, will be on hand to help the bereaved relatives; who, when a marriage breaks up, will offer friendship to both parties; and who are always willing to cut sandwiches or make tea at parish events. They do not see themselves as anything special, and brush aside any words of thanks, saying that they enjoy what they do. Yet they are the spiritual heart of the community and everyone in the village knows who they are.

Of all the various lay ministries on which the church depends, the pastoral care provided by the Mothers' Union and similar bodies, and by informal bands of good neighbours, is far and away the most valuable. It turns a parish into a community and, far from threatening the parson's ministry, it fulfils it. It demonstrates in action what the parson says from the pulpit, and it gives flesh and blood to the parson's own pastoral activities. Thus, for example, when a woman has just lost her husband, the parson can offer her the assurance of God's loving mercy, and thus be a source of great comfort and courage; yet she needs to feel that divine love hour by hour through the quiet, undemanding support of her neighbours.

Once we recognise the importance of this lay pastoral ministry, the question arises as to how best to strengthen and sustain it. Just as the lay pastors in the Bible were designated as 'widows', a term which conferred great dignity, many believe that lay pastors today should be given a title. This would both affirm their ministry, and give them greater spiritual authority in the eyes of others. Indeed, as we have already mentioned, some dioceses already encourage parishes to nominate such people to the office of 'elder' or, indeed, of 'lay pastor'. Equally, there is a strong case for offering lay pastors training, so that they can realise the full potential of their spiritual gifts. After all, if theological colleges offer courses in pastoral skills to ordinands, the laity involved in similar work should enjoy the same opportunity.

In some parishes training and authorisation of lay pastors have proved enormously fruitful. The training courses are usually quite informal, involving a great deal of discussion: since those undertaking the course have been acting quite spontaneously as pastors for many years, the purpose is to reflect on their experience rather than absorb new knowledge. Indeed, it is most important that the course should require no written work or special reading, since there is no connection whatever between academic ability and pastoral insight. Moreover, it is usually an error to use modern techniques such a role plays or 'trust games', which some people can find quite frightening. The best approach is simply to take one topic at a time, such as bereavement, marital difficulties, chronic pain, or depression, and, after a brief introduction, allow people to share their experiences and perceptions. The skill of the parson leading the course lies in drawing people out.

Parishes or, more commonly, groups of parishes which have run such courses sometimes open them to anyone who wishes to come. If the eventual purpose is to authorise particular people as lay pastors, this can be both embarrassing and hurtful, since inevitably some of those attending the course will not be chosen. The process of authorisation should have two stages, one before and one after the course. In the first stage the parish must invite people to become lay pastors. The procedure which seems to work best (and which conforms to that described in Acts 6) is for anyone, including the pastor, to be free to talk confidentially to someone whom they consider suitable; if that person agrees, the name is put to the PCC. Since everyone in a village will already know the nominees well, there is no need for embarrassing discussion of their merits and faults; five or ten minutes of quiet prayer, followed by a secret ballot, is best, and this emphasises to all concerned that it is God's will, not personal preferences, that counts.

The second stage, coming after the course, is the authorisation itself. Some people, having reflected on the responsibilities of lay pastorship during the course, may decide that they should not be appointed. They should feel free to make that choice, without any sense that they are letting down the parish, and no moral pressure should be used. But those who are willing to go forward should be authorised in a formal service in church. Many dioceses now encourage lay pastorship, with the bishop himself conducting the service, and this episcopal approval makes clear to the parish that the lay pastors are not simply the vicar's helpers, nor are they subservient to the PCC; they, like the parson and the churchwardens, must exercise their own independent judgement, subject only to the bishop's authority.

While in many parishes the training and authorisation of lay pastors can greatly strengthen the church's ministry, in other parishes it can seem cumbersome and even harmful. Some of the finest pastors would hate to be picked out for special recognition, and their quiet, hidden ministry would be inhibited if it became official. By the same token, if the Mothers' Union, or a similar body, is already acting as a corporate pastor, there is no need to appoint particular people. A more fundamental anxiety is that every Christian is called to show concern for the needs of others, so choosing some as pastors seems to devalue the ministry of the rest. Of course, in theory this should not happen, since those designated as pastors should be a focus and encouragement of the common ministry, yet in practice a system of lay pastors within a small community can prove divisive and disabling. Thus the parson and the PCC must consider the needs of their parish with great care and sensitivity before introducing lay pastors.

There is, in fact, a simple test of the state of lay ministry within a parish, and thence of whether lay pastors are required: the 'Interregnum Test'. The PCC should ask itself how the parish coped in the last interregnum. The churchwardens, any readers and the PCC itself no doubt managed splendidly: they had clear jobs to do, and set about them with vigour and enthusiasm. But the PCC should look below the surface to see whether the sick and bereaved were visited, and if families in difficulty were supported. If too many people fell through the pastoral net, official lay pastors are probably needed. If not, then the PCC should give thanks to God for the saints in their midst.

HOW MANY CLERGY CAN WE AFFORD?

In the early 1960s the Church of England ran a recruiting drive to persuade more men to offer themselves for the priesthood. Tens of thousands of posters were printed, and were pinned up on church notice-boards and even in the front windows of the faithful. They did not, however, appeal directly to potential ordinands; a picture of the Archbishop of Canterbury pointing outwards, with the words 'Your Church Needs You', would have been considered rude. Instead, we were urged to put the matter into God's hands. Thus the posters bore the slogan: 'Pray for more clergy; pray more for clergy.'

Assuming that people heeded the posters' request, then God has proved unresponsive. Over the past thirty years the number of paid clergy has dropped by about a third, and in the countryside the fall has been even steeper, with many areas losing as many as half their parsons. Indeed, it has been estimated that since 1918, when the decline began, the typical deanery in the countryside has lost one clergyman every fifteen years. At present we are on a ledge on the downward slope, with clergy numbers roughly stable in most places, but unless there is a sudden surge in vocations then numbers will continue to fall over the next few years due to retirement and death.

Behind the poster lay the belief that God wants a larger army of men in dog collars, that more equals better; and the church authorities continue to act on this belief. Unlike private industry, where a firm tries to achieve the maximum results with the minimum work-force, the Church of England is willing to consider for ordination anyone who offers themselves; if they prove suitable, it will train them, and then employ them for the rest of their lives. In years when the number of fresh ordinands rise, bishops express joy; and when the number falls, they urge more people to come forward. It is an attitude to manpower which created the bloated bureaucracies of communist countries, and which used to prevail among socialist local authorities in Britain. But while even the most ardent left-winger has rejected such a method of running the economy, it is barely questioned in ecclesiastical circles. Churchmen blithely assume that the money will be forthcoming to pay for whoever our bishops ordain.

Historically there is little justification for such optimism.

During most of the past millennium the key to the quantity (and, to some degree, the quality) of parish clergy has not been the number of vocations, but the resources to support them. Indeed, for long periods there have been more ordained people than jobs, a situation that persists in America. This has led not only to poverty and destitution amongst the less fortunate clergy, but also to all manner of abuses.

From Norman times until the early part of this century the church had two main sources of income. The first was glebe land which over the centuries had been bequeathed to the Church. In some villages this was as little as a few acres, while in others it might comprise a quarter or more of the entire parish. The second was tithes, which were a proportion of the village's annual harvest. Glebe and tithes together provided ample resources for a parish priest, and even one or two assistants, in every village, but unfortunately it rarely worked out like that. In most parishes powerful patrons took over the glebe and the right to collect tithes, and then employed curates to take services on their behalf. At the same time large numbers of impoverished young men offered themselves for ordination in the hope of improving their lot. The consequence was that patrons needed to pay only a pittance to their curates, and these curates were often so poorly educated that they could barely read the service books, let alone expound the Scriptures. The Reformers in the sixteenth century made sterling efforts to remedy this dire situation, but it continued well into the eighteenth century.

In the nineteenth century two factors combined to improve matters. First, and most important, was that Parliament finally decided to overhaul the system of patronage, and abolish pluralism. Secular patrons retained the right to appoint the parson, but could no longer appropriate the parish's income; this had to go entirely to the parson himself, and to any curates he might appoint. Moreover, the parson had to live in the parish which he served. Thus for the first time since the Saxon period every parish had its own priest. Secondly, the price of crops, and hence the rent from land, rose rapidly, reaching a peak around 1870. This enabled the clergy in even quite poor parishes to restore their churches, build substantial vicarages for themselves, employ one or two servants and even have money left over to found a village school. The middle years of Queen Victoria's reign were undoubtedly the high summer of rural ministry, from which our collective memory of the church 'as it ought to be' derives. Yet even then only a minority of the clergy actually had parishes; large numbers eked out a miserable livelihood writing letters for illiterate businessmen, coaching reluctant teenagers in Latin and Greek, and taking services when a parson fell sick or went on holiday.

This Victorian summer was, however, soon blotted out by a major agricultural depression. In the last two decades of the nineteenth and first decade of the twentieth centuries crop prices and land rents plummeted. In East Anglia an acre of prime land, which in 1880 fetched around £25 per year, was by 1910 worth barely £3. Entire farms were abandoned, their barns allowed to fall into ruins and their fields to be overwhelmed with thistles and briars. The worst casualties were, of course, the farm labourers, who were either thrown out of work altogether or forced to accept starvation wages. But parsons too, especially in the smaller villages, were cast from modest affluence to genteel poverty in a single generation, and by the outbreak of the First World War some had felt compelled, like the farmers, to abandon their livings, leaving their solid rectories gaunt and cold.

Despite a brief resurgence in agriculture during the war itself, prices and rents soon fell again in the depression of the 1920s and 1930s. It became clear to bishops and patrons throughout the country that, although there were still ample clergy to fill every parish, there was no longer the money to pay them, so financial pressure forced them to start the process of merging parishes into groups under a single parson. Fortunately, private education was now booming, which mopped up most of the surplus clergy as teachers, so the destitution of former years was avoided. The bishops for their part, far from praying to God for more clergy, were relieved that he seemed to be prompting fewer men towards ordination.

This new stringency brought the beginnings of a revolution in church finances, a revolution whose full effects are only now being felt. Dioceses began to levy a tax or quota on individual parishes. At first this was small, contributing only to diocesan expenses, but as the income from land fell further so larger amounts were needed to augment clergy incomes. At the same time the central authorities were trying to streamline the church's assets. All land and other wealth which the church as a whole owned had long since been taken over by the Church Commissioners. In addition, dioceses transferred glebe land from the individual parish to their own control, putting the rents into a common pool. As a result the parish clergy began to receive their income in the form of a monthly salary from their diocese. These salaries came from three sources: the Church Commissioners' contribution to the diocese; money from glebe land and other diocesan assets; and the quota paid by parishes to the diocese.

This broadly remains the system, but the relative importance of these three sources has undergone dramatic change in recent decades. In particular, income from the Church Commissioners and glebe has fallen as a proportion of the whole, while quota payments have been forced inexorably upwards. Moreover, in an attempt to boost the finances of urban dioceses, which have virtually no glebe income, the

Church Commissioners have frozen in money terms their contribution to rural dioceses, so inflation gradually erodes its real value. Currently in most rural dioceses the quota, or 'parish share' as it it sometimes euphemistically called, pays between a third and a half of the cost of the clergy and, while the Church Commissioners' contribution remains frozen, a fairly easy calculation can show that the quota will continue to rise at about double the rate of inflation, whatever that happens to be.

Diocesan authorities are loath to make any connection between the money which a village pays in quota and the portion of a parson's services it enjoys. This is partly in defence of an ancient principle that the vicar's stipend is independent of the work he performs: parishioners cannot therefore order him to do and say what they want, on the grounds that they pay him. It is also to preserve justice between parishes, each receiving clerical ministry according to need, not according to what they can afford. Not surprisingly, therefore, most laity also refuse to connect their quota with their vicar. In one breath they will tell the bishop or archdeacon how much they resent paying their quota, and urge that it be lowered; and in the next breath they denounce as iniquitous any idea that their parish be put into a larger group. Just as citizens the world over want to pay low taxes and yet receive lavish public services, church-goers too want vicars on the cheap.

Yet this elaborate deceit is no longer tenable, and is becoming a major stumbling-block in the renewal of rural ministry. The brute fact is that the quota now places an almost intolerable burden on many country churches, and the weight can only grow heavier in the years to come. To pay its quota and maintain its ancient building a parish must fill the calendar with fêtes, coffee mornings, gym-khanas, jumble sales and even wine-tasting parties, so every regular worshipper, as well as anyone who occasionally slips into a service, is pressed into service as a fund-raiser. The rest of the village can therefore come to regard the church, not as a source of comfort and help, but as a high-class beggar constantly on the scrounge. Aware of the treadmill, most dioceses have appointed a 'Stewardship Advisor', who visits parishes urging people to give money freely, without need of any elaborate events. However, as the Advisor elucidates the morality of stewardship, that all money and time are gifts from God to be used in his service, parishioners cannot help asking whether paying the quota is how God wants them to spend their hard-earned cash.

That awkard question, if tackled honestly, can enable both diocese and parish to look afresh at their entire approach to rural ministry. There is in truth a direct connection between the size of the quota and the number of paid clergy. In most rural dioceses the quota could be eliminated entirely if the number of paid clergy was cut by forty per cent, and the quota could be halved with a twenty per cent cut in clergy numbers. It is not impossible that such cuts may be forced on some dioceses, if substantial numbers of parishes start defaulting on their quotas, but it would be far better if the choice were clearly faced and calmly made. Parishes should ask themselves whether they would be willing to accept a smaller portion of their parson's time in return for a reduced quota, and bishops and archdeacons should encourage such questioning, and listen with care to people's responses.

People's first reaction is to fear that reducing clergy numbers still further will put the final nail in the church's coffin; yet, as we have seen, the effect could be quite the reverse. Villages today contain numerous men and women with both the ability and the education to take responsibility within the church, managing its practical affairs, conducting worship, and offering spiritual solace; and, if they were released from the treadmill of fund-raising, they would have time to devote to these tasks. Far from weakening the church's ministry, this could enormously strengthen it. As for the paid clergy themselves, they too would be released from their current role as inefficient managers, to give themselves wholeheartedly to their true calling as apostles.

4

BUILDING

IS THE CHURCH THE PEOPLE OR THE BUILDING?

The bane of the country parson's life is the fabric appeal. The architect's inspection every five years is likely to reveal several thousand pounds' of repairs to be done on each church, and from time to time there are major projects, such as releading a roof or underpinning a chancel arch. In a large group of churches there are therefore one or two appeals for money virtually all the time. A few parsons, with entrepreneurial flair, thrive on the challenge, spending many happy hours at their word processors writing begging letters to rich benefactors, former parishioners and charitable trusts. But to most parsons that large thermometer beside the churchyard gate, indicating how much has still to be raised, is an object of dread.

Small wonder that country parsons can often be heard to say, in plaintive tones, 'Surely the church is the people, not the buildings,' and they muse that their own ministry, and the life of the church as a whole, might be enhanced if a third or a half of those ancient piles were abandoned. People could then worship in each others' homes, as the first Christians did, or travel to a central church serving the whole group. Archdeacons and bishops often display great sympathy with such speculations, opining that the rural church is lumbered with 'too much plant'.

Yet if a word of these private thoughts leaks out of the vicarage, there is universal outrage. Even if only two or three people come to worship at the village church on Sunday, the entire population will rise up in protest to prevent it closing. Vicars and archdeacons have come away pale and shaking from meetings called to discuss closure plans, as if they had been mauled by wild beasts, and mild and gentle parishioners, who in normal circumstances barely raise their voices above a low drone, have made themselves hoarse expressing their anger. To them the church is not some warm and vibrant body of believers (which, as they do not hesitate to point out, barely exists within the village); the church, purely and simply, is the building. Moreover, the church turns the village itself into a community; in the oft-repeated phrase, 'a village is not a village without a church'.

The awkward truth, as so often in village affairs, is that both sides are right. To the faithful follower of Jesus, the church is and must be the people. If the church flourished and multiplied in its first three centuries without a single building of its own then it could surely survive today if it were deprived of its buildings. The mutual support of fellow disciples, and the grace and comfort of the Holy Communion, are the same in a simple farmhouse parlour as in a glorious medieval edifice.

Yet behind that staunch defence of the edifice there are important spiritual and emotional truths, which parsons ignore at their peril, and which, if lovingly embraced, can actually deepen the church's ministry. First and foremost in the hearts of local people is that the church building embodies the village; to use a Christian term, it is the 'incarnation' of the community. Indeed, the history of the community is contained in its architecture. The first church was probably built in Saxon times, soon after the village itself formed, and its foundations lie beneath the pews in the nave. The Normans then built a larger structure, in the shape of a long, high box, with a short, square-ended chancel at the east end. Some of their stonework may still be visible, such as a few round-arched windows or perhaps the chancel arch itself; yet even if none can be seen, part of the original Norman walls probably survive above the nave arcades, hidden behind plaster.

In the following four centuries the church was expanded in all directions, each generation leaving its distinctive mark, to give us the structure that we see today. Aisles were built, not to provide extra seats for expanding congregations (the English have never been ardent church-goers) but to serve as side chapels where masses could be said for the dead. The old thatch roof, which required a steep pitch, was replaced with lead, needing only a shallow pitch, and this enabled the nave walls to be raised and clerestory windows put in near the top. The chancel was lengthened to permit more elaborate rituals, and the floor raised to symbolise the importance of the Mass. As both the stonemason and the glazier grew more skilful, larger windows were installed, with delicately carved tracery and magnificent stained glass. All this work was financed both by the lord of the manor and by the ordinary peasants through the payment of tithes – ten per cent of their crops – to the church coffers. No doubt at times they resented the costs, as villagers today sometimes resent the fabric appeals which constantly make demands on their generosity. But then, as now, the dominant emotion was pride in the beauty and glory of their divine edifice.

Contrary to popular belief, work did not end at the Reformation, but turned to furnishings and fittings. Pulpits were installed from which ministers could deliver long sermons, and pews installed in which the people could

listen. Boards were put up showing the Ten Command-
ments, the Lord's Prayer and the Creed. Bells were hung
in church towers, both to call the faithful to worship, and
to indulge in bell-ringing contests, a favourite sport in the
seventeenth and eighteenth centuries. Unfortunately, the
clergy and the people were often lax in maintaining the
walls and roof, but this was remedied in the nineteenth
century when almost every village church underwent extensive restoration.

We may today be less overtly religious than our ancestors, and in our cities there is widespread indifference to
the fate of local churches, many of which have a far shorter
history. But in our villages devotion to the fabric and furnishings of our ancient places of worship is almost undim-
med. Anyone who has lived in a village for more than ten
or fifteen years will have participated in at least one major
appeal, buying raffle tickets, eating sausage rolls, and rum-
maging through jumble in order to relead the roof or
repoint the walls. Village people today continue to feel
that the church bears their mark, and so represents their
common life.

Neither should the importance of the churchyard in these
emotions be underestimated. The memorial stones bear
witness only to those buried in the last century or two.
Before that, bodies were laid in the earth with only a shroud
around them, and only a wooden cross above, so after
thirty or forty years, when the cross had rotted and the
body decomposed, the land could be redug. Thus God's
acre around the church bears the entire community for
over a thousand years; and, if the churchyard remains
open, as is the case in most villages, those who die today
are still generally buried there. Small wonder that even
newcomers to a village, who may deny any religious belief,
soon come to regard the churchyard as sacred.

Even if the parson is inclined to dismiss these feelings as

mere 'folk religion', however, there are more specifically Christian reasons for conserving ancient churches. Just as among the Hebrews the Covenant Box and, later, the Temple in Jerusalem symbolised the presence of God in their midst, so the church is a sign of God within the village. It is, in the wider sense of the word, a 'sacrament', an outward and visible sign of God's inward and invisible grace, and it reaches far more hearts than do the formal sacraments of Communion and Baptism. While only a handful receive the bread and wine each Sunday, the majority of people experience the beauty of their church as divine. When they walk past it taking the dog for a walk, when they see its tower against the setting sun, when they hear its bells chiming across the rooftops, they have a sense of the numinous, of a spiritual dimension to their daily existence.

Of course, most people never take this religious perception any further, but there are some for whom the sacrament of the village church actually becomes the gateway to faith. They want to know more about the divine being who seems to hover around the church, they feel the need to imbibe that spirit of holiness embodied in those old, grey stones, and as a consequence they start tentatively coming to the worship which takes place inside its walls. Soon the austere beauty of the building combines with the simple grace of the services to carry them to a genuine faith in Jesus.

One can add two further, perhaps negative, Christian purposes in preserving village churches. Whenever a village church is closed at least half (and usually near three-quarters) of the congregation stop worshipping, refusing to go instead to services elsewhere. It could be argued that their faith must have been weak, to have been so dependent on a particular building, but this is all the more reason for hanging on to them: it is those who are weakest in faith that Jesus most wishes to embrace. In any event, once the church is lost, so common worship in that village disappears. Moreover, the church, unless taken over by the Redundant Churches Fund, can never be resurrected, so if the village expands in a later generation, the present generation will be cursed for its mean spirit.

When a parish looks back on a major fabric appeal people often remark how rewarding it was, not only in the money raised, but also in the spirit it generated. The congregation are drawn closer together by their common purpose. As they sit together making sandwiches for the fête, as they stand together pouring hundreds of cups of tea, they are soon nattering and ribbing each other as if they were members of the same family. As they debate what price to charge for home-made cakes and jam, and as they argue over the relative merits of holding a dance on a Friday or Saturday evening, they learn each other's foibles and weaknesses. Even when at the end of a noisy jumble sale someone loses his temper, the others are given an extra insight into his personality! In church on Sunday it is possible to wear a mask; under the pressure of a fabric appeal, every mask eventually slips.

Nevertheless, clergy rightly complain that the fabric appeal may become a kind of idolatry: people can seem to worship the building itself and the money raised on its behalf, while the actual services that happen inside it are pushed into second place. Indeed, people are often far more willing to raise money for a church than praise God in it. The parson himself can find that so much of his time is spent in organising fund-raising events that he barely has time to visit the sick, and must scribble his sermons in a few desperate moments on Saturday night. He is naturally tempted at times to wonder whether the spiritual life of his people, as well as his own ministry, would not be better served if some terrorist could place a bomb in the church, blowing it to pieces.

The simple answer is that the parson should not allow himself to be sucked into fabric appeals; with four or more churches under his wing, it is unfair that he should be expected to raise money for all of them. Moreover, it is not his vocation to do so: in terms of the division of ministry described in Acts 6, there should be others responsible for the material life of the church. He should, of course, give his warm blessing to the sterling efforts of the church-wardens and PCC, and wherever possible appear at the fund-raising events, but apart from that he should, like the apostles, devote himself to the spiritual service of his people. This will give him the detachment and authority to warn people against ecclesiastical idolatry, making themselves unwitting slaves to the building, and to urge them instead to see the greater glory of God as the sole and ultimate object of their efforts.

HOW SHOULD WE USE OUR ANCIENT PILE?

A village can divide into hostile factions, as bitter as those which Paul describes in the Corinthian church, over whether three pews should be removed from around the font to make space for serving coffee, or whether the altar should be taken from the sanctuary and placed on the chancel steps. The impetus for change usually comes from the vicar, backed by a body of loyal supporters who are either convinced by his radical ideas or swayed by personal friendships for him. Then to their horrified amazement a great phalanx forms to oppose them, usually comprising an unholy alliance of more conservative church-goers and agnostic newcomers who oppose all change to their adopted village. As battle is joined, each side asserts that fundamental spiritual and aesthetic principles are at stake, and the vicar may even hear himself saying that his entire ministry is 'on the line'. Unless calmer counsels eventually prevail, a consistory court may be convened at which the diocesan chancellor, in wig and black robes, passes judgement – and the losing side is left with a fat legal bill.

The use and layout of our churches is, of course, a matter of taste and fashion, and the liturgical theories of one age are an abomination to the next. As with all fashions, if you are willing to wait long enough your own ideas will eventually come back into favour – although ecclesiastical fashions can take as long as three hundred years to be revived.

Prior to the Reformation a screen, usually made of wood and decorated with pictures of the saints, divided the chancel from the nave. The priests celebrated the Eucharist away from the eyes of the people, using Latin which was unintelligible to all but the highly educated. On top of the screen was a loft where the choir stood, although many small rural churches could not afford to pay singers. The nave was completely bare, apart from a stone ledge around the wall where the elderly and infirm could sit. Thus the worshippers enjoyed neither comfort nor comprehension, but were supposed to stand in silent awe at the mystery of the Mass. The division of the church also served to separate the sacred from the secular, so the nave could be used during the week as a meeting hall where pigs, cattle and corn could be traded, and even feasts held; indeed, there were numerous complaints that deals were struck and ale drunk even during services on Sunday.

The Protestant reformers sought both to incorporate the people into the worship, and abolish the distinction between the sacred and the secular; all life, they believed, should be sacred. So the screen was torn down, pews installed, and a pulpit erected. There was, however, hot dispute over the way in which Holy Communion should be conducted, and thence the position of the altar and the use of the church. The High Churchmen wanted to preserve the old emphasis on mystery, and believed that the altar should be kept against the east wall of the church, with the clergyman having his back to the people. There should then be wooden rails at which the people kneel to receive the sacrament. The floor of the chancel should be one or two feet higher than the nave, and the area behind the rails, which they called the sanctuary, higher still, so that the altar was the visual focus of the entire church.

The Puritans, by contrast, wanted the large altar thrown out, and replaced by a small Communion table. This should stand at the east end when not in use, but should be brought out into the middle of the chancel for Communion. The minister should stand on the north side of the table, with the people in a circle around the chancel. The floor of the whole church should be at the same level. Thus in effect they divided the church into two rooms. In the first part of the service (the 'Ante-Communion' up to the offertory) both minister and people were in the nave. The minister led the service from a stall on the south side of the chancel arch, and walked across to the pulpit on the north side of the arch to preach his sermon. Then at the offertory both minister and people walked up into the chancel to gather round the table for Communion. The emphasis was thus not on the mystery of God, but on our fellowship in Christ.

After the Restoration in 1660 a rather odd compromise prevailed. Most churches kept their small Communion table, but used it like an altar, with it firmly against the east wall during Holy Communion, and altar rails were installed in front of it. Yet despite this apparent victory for the High Churchmen, Communion was rarely celebrated, and the stress in worship was on preaching. The successful parson who attracted large congregations had a gallery erected around the nave to provide extra seating, cutting large holes in the aisle pillars to carry the joists. He also built for himself a large pulpit, with a heavy sounding-board that sat like a halo above. And, except in rare instances, the chancel and sanctuary were no higher than the nave, so the pulpit dominated the interior of the church.

True to form, almost exactly three centuries after the Reformation medieval styles swung back into fashion. The Tractarian movement, inaugurated by Keble and Newman in the 1830s, sought to restore a sense of mystery to worship, and in the following fifty years almost every church in England, including those in most villages, were in some degree affected by its teaching. The chancel and altar floors were raised. In many instances the small Communion table was shunted to the back of the church to carry a flower vase, and was replaced by a far larger altar, spanning six feet or more across the east wall. In some cases a screen was put across the chancel arch, although it usually had sufficient openings for the congregation to see the parson. Choirs, too, were revived, but instead of sitting in a loft above the screen, they were given new stalls in the chancel. The large pulpits were often dismantled, to be replaced by more modest constructions, so once more the focus was the altar at the east end.

Puritanism reach its zenith in the middle years of the seventeenth century. In the middle years of the twentieth century, three hundred years later, it too swept back into fashion – or, more precisely, some of its liturgical styles enjoyed new popularity – and, as if to prove God's sense of humour, its most ardent advocates have been Roman Catholics and High Anglicans. They have again wanted to emphasise our fellowship in Christ, so in many urban churches the altar has been moved forward to the chancel step, with the priest standing behind it, facing the congregation. This gives the impression of being in a circle, without requiring the people to shift from their pews. The sacrament is no longer received kneeling at the altar rails, but standing up: people usually file up to the front, but in more radical churches they hand the bread and wine to one another. To the devout Catholic brought up to the full splendour of the Tridentine Mass, and to the High Anglican accustomed to a distant high altar shrouded in clouds of incense, it is all most confusing. As many people have wistfully observed, Luther and Calvin would be declared saints in the modern Catholic church.

In the various gyrations of fashion the village church has, needless to say, lagged behind. While urban and suburban churches are gripped by the latest liturgical fad, village congregations are still stubbornly resisting the last fad, and when they do finally bend they make only the most minimal concessions. Thus over the centuries village liturgy has displayed remarkable stability, and as a consequence village churches have suffered fewer alterations in the interior furnishings. In a remarkable number of rural parishes the old Communion table is still in use, dating from the early seventeenth century; but it is kept firmly against the east wall, with altar rails in front dating from the eighteenth century. In a few remote places even the medieval chancel screen, resplendent with pictures of saints and a loft for the choir, survived the depredations of the Reformers. Village liturgy could best be described as High Puritan: village people like ritual in their services, but it should be simple and unfussy, and the interior furnishings and layout reflect this.

The stability of rural worship is due in part to the innate conservatism of country folk, a fact that George Herbert noted with affectionate approval in the seventeenth century; but it can be explained too by the very different challenges and problems facing country churches. In a large town the church is constantly striving to attract an indifferent population to its services, so it must be far more sensitive to the prevailing fashions and tastes of society as a whole, adapting its own style accordingly. Indeed, one can precisely match changes in liturgical style with shifts in secular culture. In a village, by contrast, the church is part of people's lives, standing in the centre of their community, and thus commanding their loyalty. The task, therefore, has been (and still is) to turn that natural loyalty into religious faith.

This does not, however, mean that nothing should ever change in the conduct of liturgy and the way in which the church building is used. Rather, rural churches must make such judgements by their own criteria. Faced with the spiritual needs which we explored in Chapter 2, rural churches today face at least three important challenges in this sphere: how to encourage informality in worship while preserving tradition; how to create an atmosphere of intimacy within a small congregation while retaining dignity; and, in some eyes most important of all, how to make the church comfortable for people accustomed to central heating and soft furniture at home.

There is no doubt that the present way in which many village churches are used is unsatisfactory. Most ministers conduct the first part of the service from a stall just beyond the chancel arch, on the south side. Yet in a large church, with the small congregation near the back of the nave, he is already very lonely; and since the stall probably faces directly across the chancel, or even in some instances due east, he is not even looking at the people when he speaks. But worse is to come after the offertory: marching up the long chancel to the altar, he becomes little more than a speck in the distance to his fellow worshippers. All this is a half-hearted and half-baked imitation of what happens in town churches – or, more correctly, what used to happen fifty years ago. As a school report might say, we 'could do better'.

Broadly there are three radical options, each of which has advantages and snags. The first is a variation on the medieval pattern. A screen is once again constructed across the chancel arch, with glass going right to the top, and wide double doors at the bottom. On normal Sundays the entire congregation sits in the chancel, which is small enough to be adequately heated and which brings parson and people close together. On major festivals and at weddings and funerals the double doors are opened, and the congregation sits in the nave. If the pews are taken out of the nave, and replaced with moveable chairs, the nave can also serve as a village hall, thus restoring the old distinction between the sacred and the secular parts of the church. This scheme can work very successfully, and indeed does so in a church in Bedfordshire where penury forced the PCC to hand the nave over to the Redundant Churches Fund, keeping only the chancel for regular worship. The main objections, apart from natural suspicion of clergy, are that people today instinctively regard the whole church, and the churchyard around it, as sacred; and also that a nave which is not habitually used for worship can easily become rather bleak, dark and forbidding.

The second radical approach is to follow many Roman Catholic churches in moving the altar to the chancel step. This too brings the parson nearer the people, while retaining the nave in use. It is the solution favoured by many Anglican clergy of more Catholic leanings. Within most village churches, however, it does have major drawbacks. Very often the chancel arch is too narrow for anything more than a small table, and even then a rotund priest would have difficulty squeezing round. Without major alterations to the floor levels, it is also impossible to provide a rail at which people can kneel when receiving the sacrament; they are therefore forced to receive standing up, a practice which most rural Anglicans dislike. A further problem is that, just as a new chancel screen can turn the nave into dead space, an altar at the chancel arch can make the chancel and sanctuary seem rather ghostly.

The third sweeping change would be to revert to the Puritan style: to use the nave for the first part of the service and then for the whole congregation to go up to the chancel at the offertory. A variation on the strict Puritan practice is for the altar or Communion table to remain in the sanctuary, while the congregation sit in stalls or chairs in the chancel; this seems to have been the method favoured by Geórge Herbert and Nicholas Ferrar. While a few youthful congregations relish this physical activity in the middle of the service, for the elderly and infirm it is an undeserved penance.

Fortunately, there is a compromise which goes some way to solving the problem without undue upset. The parson should make the first move by bringing a seat down into the nave, and placing it near the front pew: this is where he conducts the first half of the service. If there is a substantial congregation he can preach from the pulpit; if not he can stand, or even sit, in the aisle facing the people. The congregation for its part should move nearer the front, so there are only a few feet between parson and people. In most instances this brave act can be accomplished if one or two key members, such as the farmer and his wife who have been attending the church for half a century, agree to come forward. Then at the offertory, while the collection is being taken, the parson moves to the sanctuary from where he leads the Communion. This sudden distance between parson and people creates a dramatic and satisfying contrast, emphasising the holiness and mystery of the Eucharist. At the administration of the sacrament the people come up as normal, and afterwards the parson returns with the people to the nave.

There is, of course, nothing odd or peculiar about all this; it is no more than a slight variation on the traditional procedure, and it is already done in many churches. Yet by bringing parson and people close together in the nave for the Ante-Communion (and, incidentally, for the whole of Matins and Evensong) many of the styles and practices described in Chapter 2 can be enacted. Sermons can be more personal and natural, the versicles and responses can feel like real conversations, the parson can use his ordinary speaking voice, notices can be chatty with people adding their own, and hymns can be sung with gusto – there is nothing more discouraging to congregational singing than people standing so far apart that they can barely hear each other's voices. In short, by moving a few yards towards each other, parson and people can turn small into beautiful.

Another important advantage of such a compromise is that it may convince the zealous parson that his fashionable ideas – for bringing the altar forward, screening off the chancel, or whatever – are quite unnecessary. As country congregations for at least four centuries have found, new clergymen fresh from the towns need to be tamed, or else the kind of terrible hostilities described earlier will break out. If by moving from the back pews to the front the congregation can make the parson feel loved and cherished, and thus happy in his worship, they will have struck a brave blow for peace!

Parsons should be warned, however: even suggesting that people sit at the front can cause bitter argument on the PCC. It may be better, therefore, to display a serpent's cunning, as our Lord advises. The parson can simply propose that high-quality heaters are installed under the front three pews. Even if people see through the ruse, they can hardly insist that those heaters are put at the back instead.

Once the heaters are working, the battle is won. What is more, for the first time in history, people will feel comfortable in church.

CAN THE CHURCH PATRONISE LOCAL ARTS?

We have all marvelled at the exquisite frescoes that survive in so many Italian churches, and those who visit the Sistine Chapel in Rome are overwhelmed by the artistic power of Michelangelo. We are perhaps inclined to think that such vivid colour inside a place of worship is peculiar to southern Europe, while in the colder northern countries people have always preferred grey austerity.

In fact, in medieval times the walls of British churches were emblazoned with paintings. A large figure of Christ sitting in judgement looked down from above the chancel arch, with the righteous people on his right being welcomed by Peter in heaven, and the evil people on his left being cast down into hell where a gruesome Satan lay in wait. On the north wall opposite the door was a giant figure of St Christopher, the patron saint of journeys, conveniently placed so that travellers could glance into the church and offer a quick prayer to him for their safety. Round the rest of the church were scenes from the Bible and the figures of other favourite saints. Even the humblest village church was a riot of colour.

The painters were not renowned geniuses like Michelangelo, but local craftsmen who had served a long apprenticeship under a master-painter. They were not required to show originality, but to follow faithfully a pictorial tradition that had evolved over the centuries. People with quite modest talents were thus able to offer them for God's glory.

Painting, however, was only one of a number of arts and crafts which the church patronised. There were vast numbers of stonemasons who not only dressed great lumps of stone with which to build the walls, but also carved grotesque figures for gargoyles and corbels, and delicate curves and cusps for the windows. Spinners, weavers and embroiderers produced hangings for the altar, and vestments for the priests. Scribes and bookbinders made bibles and prayer-books. Carpenters gave infinite care to every detail of the choir stalls, even carving animals and abstract patterns on the misericords underneath the seats. Silversmiths and, for rich churches, goldsmiths manufactured chalices and patens for Communion, and thuribles to hold incense. Glaziers produced the most vivid pictures in stained glass so that the church seemed to blaze with colour when the sun shone. Indeed, it has been estimated that over a quarter of the entire population was involved in some way in building and beautifying churches.

The Puritans, of course, swept much of this artistry away. The walls were whitewashed and, instead of pictures, texts from Scripture were put up. Vestments and hangings were systematically seized, and either destroyed or turned into secular garments. The elaborate Communion silver was melted down, and turned into simple cups and plates without any ornamentation, the silversmith taking part of the silver as payment. The stained glass was knocked out of the windows, to be replaced by clear glass. Only carpenters were still employed in large numbers to make pews and pulpits.

In some respects English taste, especially in the countryside, remains puritanical. We prefer the walls to be white or, following a Victorian fashion, bare stone, and we want to be able to see trees and sky through some of the windows. The old Puritan fear of popery has long since disappeared, however, so while retaining an overall sense of simplicity we are happy to welcome decoration into our churches once more. In all sorts of ways the village church is again becoming the patron of all manner of local arts and crafts – or, more precisely, the church is the grateful recipient, because local people often find great joy in giving their talents for free.

The simplest project is to make kneelers, which can look remarkably fine against the wood of the pews. Various firms produce kits, where the canvas is already marked according to a standard design, and exactly the right amount of wool in each colour is provided. It is also comparatively easy for a group of people to invent original designs which in some way reflect the village and the people within it. These designs can be drawn on graph paper, and then transferred on to the canvas – numerous books are on the market which show exactly how to do it. Thus, if blackberries are rampant in the local hedgerows, a bramble branch could be depicted; a villager who enjoyed riding could show a favourite horse; a retired soldier might even want his regimental crest! The design group can ask people for ideas, and simultaneously ask for money to buy the canvas, wool and foam to put these ideas into practice. They then draw the design on to canvas, and find a willing pair of hands to stitch it. Once the project catches on, there are usually ample people happy to devote winter evenings to hassock-making; it is compatible with listening to the radio, and even keeping half an eye on the television.

A little more adventurous, but well within the scope of many people, is to produce hangings to go on the front of the altar and on the preacher's desk in the pulpit. Since these should change colour with the seasons there can be four sets: white or gold for the major festivals; purple during Advent and Lent; red for Palm Sunday and martyr's days; and green for the rest of the year. The initial materials can be quite expensive, but often people are happy to give these, perhaps in memory of a departed relative. The design group is then needed to produce a decorative pattern, bearing in mind the limitations of those who will be doing the work. A gloriously vivid effect can be achieved with quite simple embroidery and appliqué.

The technical problems of painting directly on to the walls are considerable; and besides it is extremely cold and uncomfortable to spend many hours on a scaffold, daubing paint above the chancel arch or the arcades. Yet there is no reason why a church cannot contain paintings, on canvas or wood, by local artists. In the aisles and the chancel there is usually ample wall space to put up pictures and, since they can easily be taken down again, even those who dislike them cannot condemn them as a permanent desecration! The pictures should, of course, embrace religious themes, and yet, where possible, should have local flavour too. One way of combining these requirements, much loved by medieval artists, is to depict bible stories, yet using local people's faces for the various characters, and showing local scenery in the background.

Designing and installing stained-glass windows is a highly specialised craft which even in medieval times was done in studios, the glass panels then being taken by cart to the church. Even so, quite a number of people are now learning to make small stained-glass panels, cutting different coloured glass into shapes and then bedding them in lead. These can be hung over a plain glass window, giving a dash of colour without spoiling the view.

Other possibilities for local craftsmanship in church include pottery, carpentry and lighting. There is no reason why the chalice and paten should always be made of silver, nor why the same ones should be used week after week. If someone in the village is skilled at the potter's wheel, he or she could produce a cup and plate in clay, as well as other Communion vessels such as the flagons in which wine and water are kept. Indeed, it is far more likely that Jesus celebrated the first Communion with a clay cup and plate

CAN WE AFFORD TO MAINTAIN OUR CHURCH?

If a village in Africa today wants to have a church, the people set about building it. They chop down trees to make a large frame, they cut bamboo for the walls, and they gather grass for the roof. If they want a parson, they set aside a few acres of land for him to farm, and they build him a parsonage out of wood, bamboo and grass.

This, broadly speaking, is how the village churches in England were first established in Saxon and Norman times. The people cut down trees or quarried stone for the walls of the church, and thatched the roof with straw or reeds. They then built a parsonage by the same means, and set aside a few acres, the glebe, for the parson to farm himself or let to tenants. Thus from the outset the church and the parson were supported by an endowment of land. In the early centuries there could be no collection on Sunday because the peasant had no money. But even when a collection did begin to be taken in the late medieval period, it was expected to cover no more than the incidental expenses of the church, such as candles and wine.

In the present century, however, this ancient system has suddenly collapsed. After a thousand years in which the church's endowments have maintained both her buildings and her clergy, they now cover barely half the total costs; in future decades this proportion will continue to fall. There are three major reasons for this ecclesiastical slump. Firstly, land rents as a proportion of national income have fallen from about twenty-five per cent in the mid-nineteenth century to less than two per cent today; thus the traditional source of the church's income has simply been vanishing before its eyes. Secondly, as wages have risen, so the cost of maintaining and repairing churches has rocketed: patching lead roofs, repointing stone walls, carving new stone to replace cracked tracery, and the myriad of other jobs which an ancient structure requires are all highly labour-intensive, and hence very expensive. Thirdly, the average value of stipends paid to clergy has risen. Although in the past some country parsons enjoyed considerable wealth, there were innumerable poor curates paid a pittance; today, quite rightly, all receive enough for the basic comforts of life, the current value of a stipend and free house putting them just below average income. Thus church finances have been remorselessly squeezed: income has been falling, and costs rising.

The inevitable consequence is a growing financial burden on the laity. In most rural dioceses nowadays about half the clergy stipends are paid by the laity, through the annual quota levied on parishes, and the laity is entirely responsible for the maintenance of the church building, receiving no support from the diocese or Church Commissioners. It is not uncommon for a village of three hundred souls to have a quota levied upon them of a thousand pounds or more; on top of that they must raise from among themselves the whole cost of fabric repairs. Moreover, they can no longer bodge up these repairs, as earlier generations often did. Every parish must by law employ an architect approved by the diocese, to inspect their church and supervise all but the most minor repairs; and if the churchwardens try to economise by using cheap materials and 'cowboy' builders, they can in principle be held personally liable for the cost of remedying the work.

It is hardly surprising that in small parishes clergy churchwardens and PCCs are sometimes tempted to throw up their arms in despair. Indeed, the strict regulation of church repairs gives a certain incentive for doing nothing better to leave well alone than risk incurring the wrath of architects and diocese for poor workmanship. There are some spectacular examples of the rapid consequences of such inertia. For example, a church in west Huntingdon shire was described in 1925, in the Victoria County History, as being 'in fair condition'. During the following twenty years the parish failed to clean and repair the parapet gutters of the nave, allowing water to leak into the walls. By the early 1950s the mortar had disintegrated, and the walls simply collapsed into a pile of rubble. Today only the chancel arch stands, with melancholy grace, above the brambles and ivy.

Happily, however, this story is exceptional. Most parishes show remarkable determination to keep their church standing, however many coffee mornings and wine-and-cheese evenings this requires. Churchwardens have also become increasingly well versed in the maintenance of medieval fabric, which can really be boiled down to two simple rules. The first is, at all costs, to keep the building watertight. As the parishioners in that Huntingdonshire village discovered too late, church walls are very strong when dry, but as flimsy as paper when soaked. Typically they consist of two outer skins of dressed stone, held together by rubble and lime mortar in the middle. Once water gets between the skins, the lime washes away and the outer skins fall apart. If the parish therefore does no more than make sure the gutters and downpipes are cleared of leaves twice a year, and cracks are promptly mended, it will be going a long way to preserving its church. If the roof is also checked regularly, with slipped tiles being nailed back and cracked lead being patched, many decades can pass without major trouble.

The second rule is to allow every part of the church to 'breathe'. In modern construction the interior of a building is kept absolutely dry: a damp-proof course and a membrane beneath the floor prevents rising damp, and a cavity wall prevents penetrating damp. This in turn allows us to fit carpets on the floor, and put emulsion paint and paper on the walls. Any attempt to imitate these methods in a medieval building is disastrous, however. On the contrary, the walls and floor must allow damp to pass right through them, and air must flow beneath the pews. Thus, for example, if a plastic membrane is put beneath a new nave floor, the pillars act as wicks, sucking up the trapped moisture, and soon they are covered in thick green slime. If emulsion paint is put on the walls, or polyurethane varnish on a tiled floor, it will peel off in the most unsightly fashion. If the space beneath the pews is sealed, the wood will almost inevitably rot. The answer is to use the methods and materials that our grandparents used in their own homes – it is, after all, only in this century that we have lived in bone-dry houses.

Yet however competent our churchwardens become, and however resourceful the laity are in raising funds, the battle in many villages will finally be lost if the financial squeeze continues. If the present policies continue unchanged, the average quota will almost double within the next thirty years, and many parishes will simply not be able both to meet their quota and to maintain their church. The brute fact is that there is now a direct financial conflict between paying our parsons and keeping our churches in good repair. If we insist on retaining the same number of full-time paid clergy in the countryside as we have at present, then within the next generation or two we shall have to start closing large numbers of churches. An older generation of country dwellers, which has seen the number of rural clergy almost halved within its lifetime, says in weary horror, 'there have been enough cuts in manpower'. But despite past sacrifices, the present figures simply do not add up.

One possible solution is for the rural areas to get a larger slice of the Church Commissioners' cake, at the expense of the towns and cities. Indeed, in recent years many rural bishops and clergy have pleaded for this in General Synod and elsewhere, arguing that the countryside deserves more from our 'historic resources' because it has greater 'historic liabilities' in the form of ancient, crumbling churches. Their pleas, however, seem to have gone unheard. The urban areas retort that, at diocesan level, they have far fewer endowments, in the form of old glebe land; therefore they need more from the central endowments, held by the Church Commissioners. Moreover, the typical urban clergyman already has four or five times as many souls in his patch as his rural colleague, so the scope for manpower cuts is far more limited. The inspiring and heart-rending report, *Faith in the City*, has also highlighted the poverty within many of our large conurbations. To their credit many rural parishes, in the face of such dire need, have set aside their own financial hardships, and given most generously to the Church Urban Fund. As mentioned in Chapter 3, the Church Commissioners have in fact adopted the same spirit, freezing in money terms their contributions to rural dioceses, so that inflation will gradually erode their real value, and they are increasing their grants to urban dioceses.

A second potential source of help is the government. Our ancient rural churches, as well as being much-loved places of worship, are also a central part of our national heritage. Indeed, as an island which has resisted invasion for almost a thousand years, our inheritance of medieval churches is far richer than that of any other European nation. For this reason the government, through English Heritage, has been willing in recent years to make substantial grants towards church repairs. Some argue that the government should foot the entire bill, as indeed it does in some other European countries. The bishops, however, have for many decades consistently opposed this idea, fearing that it would give the state too much control over church life: if it is paying the piper (or rather financing the concert hall) it might start calling the tune. In addition, there are more practical causes for anxiety. As any state-funded institution knows only too well, be it the NHS or British Rail, the government is an extremely fickle paymaster. Before an election it may be lavishly generous, while a year later drastic cuts are imposed. Indeed, even English Heritage has proved somewhat unreliable: in 1989, for example, it raised its level of grant, but by early 1991 funds had simply run dry. While accepting such grants as are available, it seems wiser for the church to retain its financial independence.

We are forced back, therefore, to the stark choice which we discussed earlier: either we cut the number of paid ministers in the countryside, or accept that a growing number of ancient churches will be abandoned. Surprisingly, the dilemma was anticipated over thirty years ago by A. Tindal Hart in his affectionate history, *The Country Priest*. While mourning the passing of the traditional rural parson with a single parish in his charge (which he acknowledged was largely a Victorian phenomenon), Tindal Hart robustly accepted that the money to finance him is rapidly running out. As a country parson himself, he saw that, with higher levels of education, people are better able to look after themselves without the parson's help; besides, many of his traditional roles have been taken over by the welfare state. As a result many clergymen, even with two, three or four parishes, are underemployed. He thus urged country parsons to earn some or all of their living by other means, confining their ecclesiastical activities to the weekend. This, in a nutshell, is the option we explored in Chapter 4, and it has much to commend it, spiritually as well as materially.

Unless rural dioceses grasp this nettle, and make coherent future plans, there is a danger that decisions will be made for them, perhaps in a most arbitrary and cruel fashion. As quotas rise, so some parishes will be compelled to default, paying only a proportion of the sum or even none at all. Diocesan treasurers will be forced to budget for this, adding to the quota demands on everyone else. This in turn will cause more churches to default, pushing the quota even further upward – and so on. If this nightmare is realised, dioceses will simply run out of cash to pay their clergy. Presumably they would act like most other employers in similar circumstances, failing to replace clergy who retire. Gaps would therefore quickly begin to appear quite randomly across the diocese, with groups of parishes suffering an indefinite interregnum.

Bishops and archdeacons, with their diocesan secretaries and treasurers, should not fret about this on their own. The choice must be put to deaneries and parishes as to whether they would like fewer paid clergy and a lower quota, or the same number of paid clergy and a rising quota. They should also be encouraged to explore the implications of fewer stipendiary priests: that from among the laity men and women must come forward to take greater responsibility for both the spiritual ministry and the material management of the church. If they opt for retaining the clergy, then they must commit themselves solemnly to meeting the quota which, as discussed earlier, is likely to increase by about twice the rate of inflation for the foreseeable future. If, on the other hand, they opt for a lower quota in order to preserve their buildings, then a major programme of ministerial training must be enacted as a matter of urgency. At the same time, discussions must take place with the clergy as to how best their numbers can be reduced.

Once the laity recover from the initial shock of being consulted in this way, they will respond with calm determination. Anyone who has worked in the public sector – education, local authorities, health care and the like – over the past two decades is perfectly accustomed to handling staff cuts. Those in the private sector have survived at least three recessions in the same period, so they too are familiar with economy drives. In addition, that remarkably high proportion of churchwardens who have served in the army know all about pulling back in order to regroup one's forces: a well-planned, tactical retreat is often the prelude to greater victory!

WHEN SHOULD A CHURCH BE CLOSED?

In the old coal-mining area of County Durham, a Victorian church stands perched on a hill between two colliery villages. It was built by the devout owner of the mines to satisfy the spiritual needs of his starving employees. Its very position was an insult to them, demanding that they walk over a mile, up a muddy, windswept path, to worship their Maker. It also kept the parson, who lived in a splendid vicarage beside the church, at a safe distance from the dirt and disease of the miners' cottages.

In its heyday it never attracted more than twenty regular worshippers, and since 1935, when the vicarage was sold and the church put under the wing of a nearby town, the congregation has steadily dwindled. At first a fresh-faced young curate used to cycle up the hill from the town to take services and visit people; but for the past twenty years the vicar of the town, deprived of a curate, has rushed up by car at eight o'clock in the morning, on only two Sundays a month, to rattle at great speed through Holy Communion. Now only two elderly ladies, plus a retired colliery supervisor with a voice like a siren, stagger up the hill on sunny Sundays; and when snow has fallen the supervisor comes alone.

Yet behind this quiet picture of decline a long and bloody war is being waged. In 1977 the archdeacon, with the approval of the vicar, announced his belief that the church

should be closed, and he let it be known that he would
attend the church's AGM in April to hear any views. Nor-
mally the AGM was inquorate, attracting only the siren-
voiced supervisor, but on this occasion over a hundred and
fifty men and women appeared, filling every pew in the
church for the first time in its history. The explosion of
outrage almost lifted the leaky roof, and ripe epithets of
abuse were hurled at the archdeacon which had last been
thrown at the pit owners during the miners' strike of 1926.
'This is where our people have got married and been buried
for six generations', was the essence of the message; 'It
belongs to us', and they pointed to candle sconces, altar
hangings, hymn-books and flower stands that had been
given in memory of their loved ones. The archdeacon listened, but was unconvinced. 'If you feel strongly,' he
replied, 'why don't you worship here, and maintain the
fabric?' Since that fateful day the archdeacon has made
four further attempts to close the church; each time the
outrage has been louder, once even provoking the inhabitants to mount a picket for three cold weeks when they
suspected (quite unjustly) that the archdeacon was going
to padlock the door and board up the windows. As Stanley
Baldwin once remarked, no sensible leader ever takes on
the miners.

Though expressed more delicately, parishioners all
round the country have displayed similar outrage at proposals to close their church. An archdeacon may observe
that a church has a tiny congregation, which does little or
nothing to maintain its fabric, and he may blithely assume
that local people would barely notice if the church were
abandoned. Yet when these dark thoughts are made public,
he is overwhelmed by the ferocity and vehemence of the
response, from every section of the community. Indeed, the
most pliable and sympathetic people are often the few who

actually attend worship; they may even feel relief that an impossible burden will be lifted from their shoulders.

There is, however, nothing new about closing churches. The countryside is studded with the sites of churches that were abandoned in the wake of the Black Death in the fourteenth century. Where the plague had been especially severe the surviving peasants often left their homes, and moved to empty cottages in nearby villages. As the church collapsed in the ensuing decades, people came and took the stone for other purposes, and it is often possible to find a piece of a steeple or gargoyle embedded in an old bridge or barn. Our eighteenth-century ancestors also watched a large number of churches fall, but in their case it was usually apathy, rather than illness, that was responsible. As the novels of Henry Fielding and Jane Austen attest, a cultured gentleman might lavish money on laying out a garden or putting a classical front on his residence, while the house of God beyond his gate crumbled. Even when apathy turned to zeal under Queen Victoria, ancient edifices remained vulnerable. If a church could not accommodate the liturgical tastes of the squire or parson, it was sometimes demolished, to be replaced by a new building in the desired style.

Today, when the thought arises in the mind of the archdeacon, the parson or even the people that a church should be closed, there are three questions that should be asked (there is also a fourth question that is often posed, but is strictly irrelevant). The first, of course, is how many people actually worship in it at present and whether they would be willing and able to worship elsewhere. It is important to note not just the regular attenders, but also the numbers who come to the major festivals: many country churches have as few as one or two people on most Sundays, but are full almost to bursting point at Christmas, Easter and harvest.

The second, equally obvious question is the church's capacity to raise funds. This depends mainly not on the size of the congregation but on the population of the village, since our churches are only viable if the community as a whole supports them. The recent annual accounts of the church can often give a deceptively dismal picture, since they do not necessarily reflect the village's potential. There are innumerable examples of churches which have been gently decaying for decades because neither vicar nor congregation have actually asked for money; but as soon as an appeal is launched, money pours in. Archdeacons are sometimes tempted to threaten closure if a parish is falling short on its quota but, as shrewd churchwardens often reply, if the church is closed there will be no quota payments at all. The yardstick should therefore be only its ability to maintain the fabric.

The third and toughest question concerns the future: even if the situation is bleak today, we must ask whether things could brighten in the future. Occasionally a break in the clouds is already visible, such as new housing development plans for the village, in which case it would be folly to close the church, however sparse the congregation. Usually, however, more subtle signs must be sought. If, for example, the present population is predominantly old and infirm, the next decade or two is likely to see an influx of younger families, with greater energy and resources. If the present parson is very unpopular and hence discourages fundraising, there is reason to hope that when he goes the church will spring back to life. If new industry is coming into the area, raising demand for houses, it may be reasonable to expect that the village will soon expand. When making such speculations, it is important to discover what would happen to the church after closure. If it were to be vested in the Redundant Churches Fund, it could at a later date be brought back into service, so long as the repairs undertaken by the Fund are fully reimbursed. If, however, it were to be sold for conversion into a house, or pulled down, then the decision to close it would be irreversible, which is a chastening thought for even the most hard-headed archdeacon.

The fourth question, which really should not figure in the debate, is the pressure on the parson. The clergyman with a large group, as he roars along quite country lanes from one small congregation to another, must at times wonder whether even St Paul would have approved such a mobile ministry. After the final evensong, as he slumps into his armchair, he can be forgiven for praying for a hurricane to blow down half his churches but, as we have explored earlier, closing down churches is the wrong solution to this problem. Within that group of parishes there is almost bound to be someone who could train as a reader, or even a voluntary priest, to relieve the harassed parson. In the meantime the churchwarden can read Matins and Evensong on three Sundays out of four, or the church can be reduced to one service a month when the parson comes to celebrate Communion.

Once we have articulated the questions that need to be asked, we must then determine who should respond. Discussions about closure almost invariably turn sour because the diocese takes too much authority on itself. Once people in the parish suspect that the decision will be made over their heads, they naturally resort to the language and methods of industrial action. The wise archdeacon, like the wise manager of a factory, puts as much responsibility in the hands of the people as he can afford. In particular, the first two of our three questions must be answered by the parish itself. The archdeacon or the parson can call a meeting to discuss possible closure, and simply ask the people: 'Do you believe that it is right to keep the church open with so few worshippers?' and 'Are you prepared to raise sufficient money to maintain its fabric properly?' This puts the onus squarely on the parish itself, and inevitably people will try to wriggle, shifting the blame on to the diocese for not maintaining the fabric, and even grumbling about the vicar's sermons as a reason for them not coming to services. The archdeacon and vicar must simply hold firm, explaining that by law the parish is responsible for its church, and that, as far as services are concerned, people should come to worship God not the parson.

Prophesying the future cannot be left wholly to the parish. Certainly the local people can be asked their opinions as to how the village, and its spiritual needs, may evolve over the coming few decades. But the diocese too must make a judgement, both as to whether a congregation and its finances may grow, and also as to how long the building can survive without repair. In many spheres the church is rightly accused of dithering over decisions, and thus failing to give a clear lead. On the issue of whether and when to close a church, delay is a positive virtue. The longer the evil day can be postponed, the more likely it is that some new blood will enter the parish to improve matters, or at any rate some new housing development will be approved by the planning authorities.

It is often said that when the church in a village goes, God seems to leave as well. Of course, that is not literally true, since God remains present within the most faithless community. Yet undoubtedly the village is weaker in spirit, and there is no longer a visible Christian group to which the newcomer can adhere. Moreover, when a village abandons its most precious and beautiful treasure from the past, its future is impoverished beyond measure. The closure of a church is like the extinction of a species: a long, slow evolution is suddenly obliterated. When the sword of closure hangs over a village church, therefore, it is well to remember that the present generation threatens to destroy what forty or fifty generations created.

5

MISSION

HOW CAN WE PROCLAIM THE GOSPEL IN OUR VILLAGE?

In most people's minds the words 'mission' and 'evangelism' conjure up an image of a large meeting addressed by some charismatic preacher, and regaled by enthusiastic youngsters singing choruses, the modern master of such missions being, of course, Billy Graham. We are perhaps apt to feel that, unless we too are organising similar meetings, we are not answering our Lord's call to 'be his witnesses to all peoples'. Yet when we look round our parish, it is dishearteningly clear that, even if Billy Graham spoke in the village hall on every evening for a month, the effect would be negligible. The majority of those who attend mass meetings are either already Christians, or teetering on the brink of faith. In a small village there would barely be enough such people to fill the first couple of rows, and afterwards the parson could count himself fortunate if a single extra worshipper were added to his flock.

The mass meeting is, and always has been, an urban phenomenon. It was pioneered by such soul-stirring preachers as George Whitefield and John Wesley in the eighteenth century and, although they visited numerous villages, their great success was outside factory gates and at the top of mines, where they could gather large crowds.

Both Wesley and Whitefield had voices that could carry across thousands of heads, generating passionate emotions in their hearers, while Wesley's brother Charles wrote gloriously sentimental hymns, set to tunes he had picked up in taverns and in the street, which could warm the coldest of hearts. Yet these great evangelists knew that they were not sowing the gospel on fresh ground: they saw their meetings as 'revivals', in which dormant faith was brought back to life.

Today, in towns and villages alike, the majority of people have no faith to revive. Not only do children grow up with virtually no knowledge of Christianity, but their parents and even their grandparents share their ignorance. Even in those parishes where the church is packed at harvest and Christmas, it is unlikely that more than a quarter or a third of the population is present; to the rest even simple 'folk religion' is alien. The organisers of mass missions in a town or city may persuade a few such people to come to their meetings, and the emotional force of a large crowd may prise open their hearts to the love of Christ, but even the most optimistic evangelist admits that the bulk of lost souls are beyond his reach. In a village, such meetings would fall so flat that the gospel would merely be made to look ridiculous.

Going back far beyond Whitefield and Wesley, to when our islands first embraced the Christian faith, quite different evangelistic methods were employed. In the fifth, sixth and seventh centuries even our towns were no bigger than large villages are today, and most people lived in small settlements of a few hundred souls, surrounded by dense forest. The missionaries who went first to Ireland, and thence via Scotland into England and Wales, were monks whose first act on entering a new district was to build a monastery. They cleared a few acres of forest, using the wood to construct a church and cells, and they planted crops and reared animals to feed themselves. They then usually opened a school, inviting local families to send their sons to be educated. At the same time monks went out, either singly or in pairs, to visit local villages. In each village they asked the chief man to give them food and lodging and, when they were settled, they sent word round the village that anyone who wished to know about Jesus Christ could come and see them. Once a small nucleus of believers had formed, a church was built, and one of the new Christians was sent to the monastery to train as a priest. The monks then moved on; but they returned frequently, especially in times of plague or famine, to encourage the priest and his flock in their faith.

Thus from the outset evangelism was linked with pastoral care. The monks did not simply preach to the people: they sought to make friends, and to look after those who were sick or poor, and through education they tried to instil Christian values into the new generation. The biography of St Cuthbert, written by Bede, reveals that there were frequent set-backs: when, for example, an especially nasty illness spread through the hills of Northumbria, Cuthbert found that his converts were reverting to the old pagan magic for a cure, and he rushed from one windswept homestead to another, urging them to hold fast to the power of Jesus. Despite this deep attachment to the old religion, however, the whole country had become Christian within a couple of centuries: the love and care which the monks displayed, and the same love and care which radiated from the churches they established, gradually won people's hearts.

If Cuthbert's biography provides the most vivid insight into the activities of those first monks, his older contemporary, St Aidan, bears witness to the attitudes which guided them. He was a monk at Iona when the first missionary was sent from there into northern England. After a year this pioneer returned without success, complaining that such 'an obstinate and barbarous people' would never submit to Christ. Aidan suggested that he had been too severe with his ignorant hearers, offering them 'strong meat' when they could only take 'spiritual milk'. As a result of his intervention Aidan was himself sent to England, where he indeed offered milk. He never threatened people with hell-fire if they did not believe, nor did he preach long sermons. Instead, he wandered on foot from one settlement to another, talking to everyone he met, and visiting the home of anyone whom he heard was sick. Whenever kings or chieftains gave him presents, he passed them straight on to the poor.

Despite the comparatively affluent appearance of the modern village, Aidan and Cuthbert would soon feel at home. People again cling to all sorts of pagan beliefs, from the ability of astrology to foretell the future to the power of pills and potions to cure all ills. Behind these beliefs Aidan and Cuthbert would find the same fears and anxieties that gripped the hearts of the primitive peasant. People still yearn to be part of a close-knit community, and respond warmly to anyone who shows love and friendship without passing judgement or criticism. Indeed, it is the desire for community which prompts many people to move to the countryside. Aidan and Cuthbert would thus no doubt set about their missionary task in much the same way as they did fourteen centuries ago.

We should seek to emulate them. Our position today is similar to that of our primitive ancestors, shortly after the monks had first arrived. In each village there is a small nucleus of believers, with a church building. The first priority is to find at least one person in that nucleus who can be trained as a reader or minister, to become the local leader. He or she can then inspire the Christian community to reach out in love and friendship to the village as a whole.

When someone is sick, a church member should be on hand to offer encouragement and practical help. When a marriage breaks up, a church member should be ready to hear and receive the explosion of emotion. When someone runs into financial difficulty, church members should even club together to offer assistance. The opportunities to express Christ's love in even the smallest villages are boundless and, as St Paul wrote to the Galatians, we should 'seize every chance to do good'.

There will not be instant results. Indeed, it is a form of idolatory to judge the value of Christian love by the number of extra people on pews: it is God who turns our love for others into a living faith within their hearts. Besides, if it took Aidan, Cuthbert and their saintly successors two hundred years to convert Britain, the present generation should regard itself as planting seeds for future generations to harvest. None the less, if we are devoted in our pastoral care, we shall see some signs of growth.

The most important sign is that the invisible barrier, which for many people stands across the church porch, will melt away. Those of us who walk freely in and out of church are largely unaware that, for the majority of our neighbours, there is a spiritual block that actually prevents them coming into the building. If they ever face this block, they usually ascribe it to the shortcomings of the church-goers: they are 'unfriendly' or 'hypocritical'. But in fact the barrier is their fear of Jesus Christ: they shrink from the demands he may make on their lives if they come too close to him. This is hardly surprising when one considers that Jesus requires the total commitment of his disciples: people who stay away from church may, in their own way, have a deeper appreciation of the power of Christ's cross than many worshippers. This fear can only be overcome if people can see that Jesus not only makes demands, but also gives comfort and courage; hence the joy of the Christian faith far exceeds the sacrifices. It is for the church congregation to share this comfort and demonstrate this joy by their pastoral activities within the parish.

The immediate consequence is that more people will feel able to come to the major festivals. One may also be surprised to see new faces at minor festivals such as Remembrance Sunday: ex-servicemen, for the first time in half a century, may feel drawn to thank God for their departed colleagues. If on these initial, tentative visits people experience both warm friendship and also heartfelt prayer, they may want to come more frequently. Indeed, it is astonishing, and encouraging, how many new church-goers point to the intercessions as the aspect of worship which most deeply impressed them: they were delighted to find that this small group actually bothered, week by week, to think about and pray for the sick and infirm within the village.

There is one instrument of rural mission that was not available to Aidan and Cuthbert, but can be enormously valuable today: the parish magazine. People have an insatiable appetite for local news and chit-chat, so a good parish magazine gains a wide circulation – and it is read from cover to cover, with minute attention. Parsons are liable to imagine that their 'letter', in which they try to expound their Christian faith, is the most important evangelistic element within the magazine. In fact, the missionary value of the magazine depends on the spirit of love and friendship which permeates all its pages. The good wishes expressed to those who are ill, the condolences offered to the bereaved, the congratulations extended to children who have excelled in some way, and the welcome given to newcomers are the heart of the magazine. Those who read their own names or those of their close friends will feel the care of the church reaching out to them. There is no need for the magazine to be glossy or slick, and it should never be strident or offensive. Its purpose is to be warm and sweet – 'spiritual milk', as Aidan would have said.

HOW SHOULD WE WELCOME NEWCOMERS?

The majority of inhabitants in a village were once newcomers. Out of a population of, say, three hundred, less than thirty will have been born in the village; these are in the main retired farm labourers and farmers. The elderly women will have come to the village half a century ago, to marry one of the labourers, and the rest will be people who have chosen to live in the village for its tranquillity and beauty. At least ninety per cent of rural dwellers have thus had the experience of moving into a strange community.

The pattern and rate of influx, however, vary enormously from one village to another. In a small hamlet, with no new housing, newcomers can only move in when the old residents die, so the change in the community is barely perceptible. At the other extreme are villages which have been selected by the planning authorities for rapid expansion, with entire new housing estates springing up around the edge; here, the older residents are overwhelmed by the newcomers, and the character of the village changes entirely within a few years. In between lie the bulk of our villages which have witnessed some new housing in the past twenty-five years, replacing old terraces of labourers' cottages or filling in gaps along the village street. Typically, those who move into the new houses stay for a far shorter period than the old residents, as they chase round the country in pursuit of their careers. The challenges facing the church in these different types of villages are vastly different. Where the village has remained static in size, or grown only slowly, the main challenge is for the existing congregation to offer genuine friendship to the newcomers, welcoming them into their midst. This sounds easy, but in fact can be quite tough. In a small village which has seen little change, the congregation is like a close-knit family, with its own way of doing things, its own little jokes and idiosyncrasies, and even to some degree its own way of talking. Its members may smile warmly at the newcomer, and say with sincerity how pleased they are to see a new face, but they may make no effort to draw the newcomer into their family, and see no reason to adapt themselves or put themselves out for the benefit of the newcomer. Thus, without being remotely aware of what they are doing, they shut the newcomer out; if the newcomer stops coming to church after a few weeks, it merely confirms their unconscious conviction that the younger generation has no staying power.

There are specific measures a church can take to break down this invisible wall. If lay people read the lesson, the newcomer can quickly be invited on to the rota. Equally, there is no reason why the newcomer cannot become a sidesman after a few months, preparing the church for worship and taking the collection. In many small villages the PCC consists of anyone who wishes to sit on it, so here too the newcomer can be asked to join in. There is, of course, a danger that the newcomer feels pounced upon, and then loaded with burdens which older residents are only too happy to shed; invitations should therefore be offered in such a way as to permit a refusal.

It is not, however, rotas and committees that will prise open the Christian family to the newcomer. Just as ordinary families are held together through sharing the washing-up and going out together, so practical work and social events draw people into the church family. The new member of the congregation should be asked to help with the summer fête and winter coffee evening, planning and running the stalls. Devising new games with which to fox the parishioners, sitting round a table piled high with bread to be turned into sandwiches, and standing side by side at the white-elephant stall, all awkwardness and formality soon disappear. 'Baptism by fête' aptly expresses the process of joining a village congregation.

All these lessons also apply to the larger village in which new estates have been built, where it is equally important that people are warmly received into the Christian circle. There is, however, an equal and opposite challenge in such circumstances: that the older residents should feel at home among the newcomers. When the influx is both rapid and large, the existing inhabitants can easily feel overwhelmed. Not only does the appearance and character of the village change, but they often find themselves eased off village institutions, such as the village hall management committee and the parish council. They can soon feel that there is no place for them within the village – they feel driven out. It is vital that the church does not collude with this process, but rather works hard to integrate the old and the new.

This is in part a matter of avoiding simple mistakes, which are, unfortunately, all too frequently made. In worship the newcomers may be accustomed to the more active and bustling style which has become popular in our cities and suburbs, and so may initially react against the more traditional style in the village as 'boring' or even 'dead'. It does not take many adverse remarks for the sensitive vicar or minister to feel under pressure to 'brighten things up', and once newcomers form a solid block on the PCC this pressure becomes intolerable. The older worshippers may at first concede the need for some change, in order to 'keep up with the times', but before long services have changed out of all recognition as the village apes the suburb; not surprisingly some of the older people quietly fall away, excluded from the church they have cherished for half a century. No one has deliberately sought to hurt them, and the newcomers would be deeply upset if they could peer into their hearts: with good intentions a cruel wrong has been committed.

The same unconscious cruelty can be enacted in other aspects of church life. Most village churches have an annual round of social and fund-raising events whose style and organisation have been hallowed by tradition. They are unlikely to be as exciting or as profitable as the effort expended on them warrants, but people feel comfortable with them and, with minor variations from one year to the next, know what is expected of them. The enthusiastic newcomers, as they propose radical changes to liven things up and boost profits, are unwittingly trampling over the feelings of those who have kept these events going for decade upon decade. Many private tears have been shed as the old bring-and-buy stall is cast aside in favour of a high-quality gift stand, and as the wooden skittles carved lovingly by the old churchwarden's father in the 1920s are replaced by a bright plastic set.

The parson is in a unique position to bridge the gulf between old and new. He himself is a newcomer, in that he came from outside, probably from a town, into the village; yet he holds the most ancient office within the village, and represents the most ancient institution. He is thus on both sides, and can help each to understand the other. When pressure for change is brought to bear, he must have the courage to resist it, until everyone can genuinely support it. Such delay usually enables the old and the new to grow together: the newcomers gradually learn to appreciate the traditions which at first sight seemed so dreary, and the old residents learn to sift good ideas for change from bad ones.

More profoundly, both sides will discover that beneath their conflict there is spiritual and emotional unity. In the old Book of Common Prayer the beautiful collect for the

Fourth Sunday after Easter prays that 'among the sundry and manifold changes of this world our hearts may surely there be fixed where true joys are to be found'. People have always looked to the church for a sense of stability: its steady rhythm and worship offer reassurance and comfort amid so much bewildering uncertainty, and as the rate of social and economical progress has accelerated, so this yearning for stability has increased. Moreover, in the English imagination, the village church is like a solid rock amid the crashing waves of change. Paradoxically, newcomers to the village may advocate different styles of worship and new ways of organising the church's life; but while to the older residents these proposals seem new and revolutionary, to the newcomers they are the 'traditions' which they carry with them from the suburban church. Thus, although there may be disagreements between old and new, both bring the same spiritual and emotional needs to the church.

The two can be reconciled, therefore, if they recognise that stability does not mean stasis, that traditions can grow and adapt while retaining their roots wholly intact. Thus, with care and sensitivity, the old styles of worship and the old ways of running the church can incorporate fresh ideas and visions without threatening the stability to which people cling. Indeed, the newcomer's ideas and visions can actually breathe new life into the old traditions, and so by degrees a common tradition emerges with which everyone can identify. The key to success is never to rush and never to push, but to listen carefully and lead gently; and if a wrong step forward is taken it is a sign of strength, not weakness, to admit the mistake and apologise. The village church should be a tortoise, not a hare, moving slowly enough for everyone to remain safely and securely within its embrace.

HOW SHOULD WE RESPOND TO CHANGE IN OUR VILLAGE?

For two centuries and more the villages of Britain have been forced to dance to the tune of the cities. As the factories, the 'dark satanic mills', expanded in the early nineteenth century, so the traditional crafts of the villages were overwhelmed, and the unemployed craftsmen were forced to leave their ancestral homes to seek work in the factories that had destroyed them. Later, as urban engineers invented machines to till the land and harvest the crops, so the farm labourers too were compelled to abandon their cottages and trek to the cities. Most recently, many affluent city-dwellers have bought homes in villages, commuting each morning back to the city for work, so that many villages are now little more than urban dormitories.

Today, however, the village is beginning to play its own tune, and in the decades to come that tune is likely to grow clearer and clearer, forcing the city to dance to its rhythm. Indeed, the exodus of city dwellers into the countryside is the first sign of this revolution. They are acknowledging with their feet that the huge conurbation is an unnatural and inhumane form of human settlement, that people were only forced to move there through dire poverty, and that as soon as financial circumstances allow many want to move back to the countryside. Like most other species on earth, *homo sapiens* flourishes best in small groups, where everyone knows the others personally, and thus feels an emotional bond with them. In such groups people are naturally more friendly and supportive, and far less likely to commit crimes. Thus, now as always, people regard village life as safe and secure, in which children can grow up and adults grow old in relative peace and harmony. Of course, no village conforms to the romantic image which many city dwellers possess but, by most objective measures, the quality of life is undoubtedly higher.

This retreat to the village is, however, only the opening bars of a melody, in which economics, politics and ecology will soon add their distinctive sounds. Our cities grew so huge in the nineteenth and early twentieth centuries because our factories were so vast, each employing hundreds and thousands of men and women along a giant production line. But in the past two or three decades the era of the big factory has suddenly drawn to a close, and now in most industries the most efficient factory or office is quite small. Thus the economic purpose of the conurbation has disappeared, and the areas of Britain which in recent years have enjoyed the greatest prosperity are those which offer the most pleasant and tranquil environment for small businesses and workshops.

As yet politicians and planners have barely awoken to this revolutionary economic change, but the social and geographical implications are already clear. There is growing pressure for industry to move back to the countryside, either occupying small business parks on the edge of villages or, in the case of the increasing number of 'freelance' workers, operating from people's own homes. In villages where business parks have been founded, the flood of applicants has been the envy of councillors and planners from the cities. Within the next couple of generations the population of many of our villages may double and treble, the new houses occupied not by commuters but by people who can simply walk along the village street to their work, just as they did in former times.

Agriculture is also facing a revolution, as it did two centuries ago in parallel with the Industrial Revolution. Here too there will be a return to older patterns, but with modern techniques. Farmers now mainly agree with ecologists that present methods of cultivating the soil cannot continue. Huge doses of chemicals not only pollute the waterways but also undermine the natural health of the soil, and heavy machines crush the soil's structure. Moreover, as hedgerows have been ripped up to make way for these machines, the weakened soil is now washing and blowing away. Already in certain areas yields are falling, so that farmers themselves are now open to more organic methods, in which chemicals are replaced by natural fertilisers and pesticides. This will probably lead to a small but significant increase in the number of people working on the land, again boosting local employment.

There is perhaps a third revolution which will profoundly affect village life over the coming decades, and which will also carry distinct echoes of the past. During the nineteenth century the Church of England founded a school in almost every village. In most cases the parson himself took the initiative, raising money to build a single large classroom with an entrance for boys on one side, and an entrance for girls on the other, and adjoining was a small house for the schoolmaster and his family. By the time elementary education became compulsory in 1870 almost ninety per cent of rural children were already going to school, with even the humblest family paying a small fee. The Education Act of 1944 brought these schools into the state system, leaving the Church of England only a limited degree of influence, and in the following decades, as the population of many villages declined, a large number of schools were closed.

In recent years, however, the thrust of government policy has been to push education back into local hands again, and it is quite conceivable that within the next generation each neighbourhood will again be responsible for the education of its children, with only a small degree of guidance and financial assistance from the state. While people may debate furiously as to whether such a trend is desirable, local control of education will represent an exciting challenge to the rural church to resume one of its major historic roles.

There is within the human heart a natural conservatism: we instinctively resist change even if there are compelling intellectual arguments in favour of it. We should treasure and nurture this instinct, because it holds us fast to our spiritual and social traditions. Yet merely to denounce all change as a matter of principle, without any attempt to assess its potential benefits and to guide its course, will actually hasten the pace of change and ultimately destroy our traditions. Thus, for example, the parish council which rejects every planning application for new housing will soon be ignored by higher authorities as obstructive and stupid; and so instead of influencing the shape of the village, it becomes a passive victim of the planners' whims. Equally, a church which makes no concessions to the needs of newcomers will gradually dwindle as the older residents die.

The rural church has in this context a vital prophetic role. It must try to guide the attitudes of local people, so that they can distinguish beneficial from harmful change, and to this end it must articulate the moral and social values on which such judgements should be made. It is not for the church to throw its weight behind specific proposals, such as a new housing scheme or even a tree-planting plan. Even the most apparently innocuous idea can have ardent opponents, and if the church takes one side, it will inevitably alienate those on the other. Its role is to lay bare the principles on which everyone should agree. Broadly in village affairs there are three such principles.

The first is that the village should see itself within the context of society as a whole, responding to the social, economic and spiritual needs of those beyond the parish boundary as well as those of its own inhabitants. Thus, although local people may not like the idea of more housing or a business park on the edge of the village, this in itself is not sufficient reason to oppose them. On the contrary, if a gradual dispersal of both people and jobs from the cities to the countryside is desirable for Britain, then individual villages should be willing to play their part. This means that the debate should start, not with the particular needs and problems of one's own village, but with the challenges facing the entire country. Then, when one has seen the wider picture, one can look at the place of one's own village within it.

Secondly, each village should aspire to be a living, self-reliant community. Although many commuters make a valuable contribution to village life, they would themselves acknowledge that it is wrong for a village to become a mere dormitory; no doubt many of them too would be delighted to throw their season ticket to the winds, working instead within the village – what joy to walk quietly and calmly back from work along a country lane, on a warm summer's evening! Villages should thus actively welcome new employment within the parish boundaries; their concern should be that the new workshops and offices blend harmoniously with the surroundings.

Thirdly, there should be a sense of mutual responsibility within the village, so that the interests of all the residents are taken into account. Equally, all should be encouraged to take part in any decisions and actions on behalf of the village, which is especially important when it comes to matters of social welfare, such as education. One of the extraordinary achievements of those Victorian country parsons who founded our village schools is that they attracted children from almost all the social strata. Everyone also felt responsible for the upkeep of the school buildings, raising money and doing odd jobs for nothing. If our schools revert to local control there is a danger that articulate and forceful groups of parents will dominate them, guiding the methods and content of education according to their own convictions, and thus other parents will feel excluded from influence. The church in this sphere continues to command great respect, even among those who do not subscribe to its doctrines. It can therefore play a mediating role, ensuring that every voice is heard and a common vision is found.

In past centuries, when the church as an institution articulated principles, it was the clergy alone who spoke: the church was wholly identified with its paid ministers. Today, however, most villages do not have a resident parson, and, besides, the clergy are no longer given the respect that they once enjoyed. The church must consequently exert its influence in village affairs through all its members, and it can do this in two ways. It can itself convene meetings at which particular matters are discussed: clearly such meetings would have no authority to reach decisions or pass motions, but instead their purpose would be to reflect in a leisurely and uncontentious fashion on the underlying issues. It is through such informal gatherings that fresh insights can most readily emerge, and a consensus can be discerned. In addition, Christians can and should involve themselves in secular bodies within the village that carry power and influence, such as the parish council, amenity groups, the school governing body, and so on, and on such bodies they should not be frightened to apply their moral and spiritual beliefs to practical questions. People may at times express impatience that morality is dragged into their debates, but they soon discover that, by putting matters within a moral perspective, the right practical decision is usually perceived far more quickly.

In the past fifty years or more the dominant note of the rural voice has been plaintive. Village people have grumbled about declining bus services, the closure of schools, heavy traffic along their streets, even poor sewage disposal. Not surprisingly, town-dwellers have displayed scant sympathy: they need only drive through a few villages to see that such rural problems are as nothing compared with the deprivation and disorder of many inner cities. In the coming fifty years let the rural voice speak in bright, hopeful tones. To a quite remarkable degree the future now belongs to our villages. It is in the countryside that many of the great social, economic and ecological challenges must be met, and if we rise to these challenges our villages may offer a humane and prosperous way of life to a third or even a half of the British population, from every class and background. Moreover, this dispersal of population back to the countryside will allow those who remain in the cities to breathe and move freely once again. For the church this offers a golden opportunity to be in the vanguard of progress – for the first time in at least four hundred years.

Incidentally, the growth of population may in the fullness of time allow the number of paid clergy to increase, even eventually restoring the Victorian ideal of a parson in each village. But this should happen not by diocesan fiat, but by the demands of the parishioners themselves, who would be required to put their money where their mouths were!

IS GOD GREEN?

Within less than a century of the death of Jesus, Christians were trying to delineate which areas of life were their proper concern and which they could ignore, and this effort has continued to this day. Some have tried to distinguish the spiritual from the material aspects of life, asserting that the church should address itself solely to the spiritual. Certain Christian groups have accordingly devoted themselves exclusively to prayer and meditation, often inflicting severe pain and hardship on their bodies to release themselves from material attachments. Others have used the same distinction of spirit and matter to apply themselves exclusively to saving souls, by urging people to accept Christ as their personal saviour; they too have displayed lofty indifference to material affairs, ignoring injustice and tyranny.

Another popular division is between the moral and the political spheres. The moral sphere is taken to include family life and sexuality, plus charitable activities to help the poor and needy, and in these areas the church is expected to speak with a clear, unequivocal voice. The political sphere embraces not only government itself, but economics and business; here the church is required to remain dumb. There are in this view a few points where politics and morality meet, such as the passing of laws on divorce, abortion and other such domestic matters, and in these areas politicians are usually allowed to vote freely according to their moral convictions. There are also a few grey areas, such as education, which lie largely within the political sphere but where morality has a stake. But by and large the two should be kept strictly separate.

Unfortunately, neither of these delineations of the church's social role match up with Scripture, nor do they hold up in practice. The Hebrew prophets spent much of their time denouncing the tyranny of kings and the greed of merchants, and they felt no compunction about enunciating God's plan for the state of Israel. Furthermore, while Jesus stood far above any political battles, his moral teaching applied to every aspect of human life. Sadly, in the two millennia since the death of Jesus the church has frequently deafened itself to the cries of the poor and the oppressed, and by its inaction has colluded with the perpetrators of injustice. As a result it has rightly been condemned for hypocrisy.

Today a new crisis faces our world, where politics and

morality, spirit and matter, are manifestly bound together: the destruction of our natural environment. The Book of Genesis teaches us that all animals and birds, all plants and insects, are created and hallowed by God, and that human beings are the stewards of God's creation. The Hebrew Law contained in Leviticus and Deuteronomy gives clear instruction to farmers on the care of their land, so that its fertility and abundance may be conserved from one generation to the next. If we are tempted to dismiss the fauna and flora around us as unspiritual, the opening verses of St John's Gospel remind us that the Logos, the Word of God made flesh in Jesus, is the means 'through which all things were made'. For the first time in history the church has no escape from its wider responsibility: it must speak with the prophet's voice.

The rural church is also at the sharp end of the prophetic stick for the first time in half a millennium. The most precious natural resource is not oil or iron ore or any of the other minerals on which industry depends; it is the soil beneath our feet. Every animal and every plant depends on the soil for life itself, and it is the rape of the soil which poses by far the greatest threat to our planet's future. Most of the existing deserts of the world are man-made, due to wanton cutting down of trees and bad agricultural practices, and now this nightmare is beginning to be realised even in Britain. In some regions of arable farming over ten per cent of the land is already infertile, the topsoil turned to dust, and then blown away by the wind and washed away by the rain. At the present rate the eastern counties of England will within the next century share the fate of north Africa: once the granary of the Roman Empire, intensive monoculture brought the Sahara Desert right up to its northern Mediterranean coast.

The apparent villains are the farmers. It is they, after all, who shower the soil with chemicals and crush it with their heavy machines; it is they who have pulled up the hedgerows and chopped down the copses; and it is they who sow the same narrow range of crops each year, giving no opportunity for the soil's natural fertility to recover. It is, then, tempting to see the church's job as persuading farmers to mend their ways. In each parish the parson could convene a series of meetings in which experts in mixed, organic agriculture could show the farmers how to be good stewards of the land, just as modern missionaries and workers organise such meetings in Asia and Africa.

A closer look, however, reveals that farmers are to a great extent victims of a system over which they have little control. The government, guided by the European Community, sets prices for most farm products, and offers a complex range of subsidies and incentives. The farmers for their part are mostly tenants, operating on quite narrow profit margins, and in order to survive they must work as the framework of prices and subsidies requires. Hedgerows were destroyed, for example, because a grant was given for such vandalism; crop yields are maximised, with scant regard for the long-term health of the soil, because prices are not permitted to fall in response to excess supply; mixed farming, in which animal manure fertilises the fields, has virtually disappeared because there are no financial incentives; farmers were until recently encouraged to purchase vast machines, and thence reduce their workforce, because generous capital allowances were paid. The individual farmer who courageously tried to buck the system simply went bankrupt.

The rural church, if it is seriously to foster good stewardship, has no choice but to muddy its hands in the dirty world of politics, but in doing so it must make it clear that it is not opposing the farmers, but standing shoulder to shoulder with them so that they can conserve their own livelihood. Clearly, individual parsons and parishes have neither the intellectual resources nor the influence to campaign for changes in policy. Rural dioceses, operating both singly and in concert, must therefore take the lead, organising study groups and seminars and putting forward cogent proposals for change, and they must tap all the economic, political, scientific and ecological expertise at their disposal. Too often the commissions and committees which the church convenes on political and social issues are overloaded with clergy and theologians, so their reports, while filled with scriptural and moral insight, are ·naive and unrealistic in their practical proposals. While there may be a shortage of Christian experts in many political fields, when it comes to agriculture there is an abundance of talent on every aspect, for the good reason that the Church of England remains strongest in the countryside.

The local church is far from helpless in this green revolution. As in spiritual matters, the church can exert great influence through quite small, symbolic acts. It possesses a priceless ecological asset in its own churchyard, for example. The ground between the graves is probably the only soil in the parish that has not been dug and turned in the past five hundred or a thousand years, and thus contains wild flowers and grasses that are virtually extinct elsewhere. These can be destroyed by ruthless mowing. Instead, they should be allowed to come into blossom and seed in late May and early June: only then can they be safely scythed down. In fact, ideally a churchyard should be cut only twice a year, once in mid-June, and then again in September. People will complain that the churchyard is not being kept 'neat and tidy', and that disrespect is therefore being shown to the dead, but this gives an opportunity to explain to them the principles of conservation and that the dead are contributing to the survival of our planet!

The gravestones also fulfil a valuable ecological function. The old gravestones which were slotted directly into the earth rarely stay upright, but eventually come to rest at an angle; each therefore catches the sun in a particular way, which enables different species of moss and lichen to grow, depending on the amount of warmth and light they require. Not surprisingly, the same people that advocate a closely-mown churchyard also like to see gravestones straightened, but this simple act can destroy two or three centuries of growth. Instead, the people of the village should be encouraged to peer closely at those familiar monuments: they will discover a veritable museum of rare plants clinging to the stones, each with its unique colour and texture.

If farmers are trapped in an economic system constructed by politicians, individual households within the village are free to use their own patch of land as they please. Christians, eager to promote the green message of the Bible, can therefore learn to become organic gardeners. Indeed, it would be sheer hypocrisy to urge a green revolution in agriculture while continuing to spray toxic chemicals in one's own backyard. There are now innumerable excellent publications for the green gardener, explaining the mysteries of compost, vegetable rotation, interspersing crops to deter pests, and so on. One soon discovers that organic methods require great skill and knowledge which many modern farmers unfortunately no longer possess, so by applying such methods at home the Christian acquires both greater sympathy for the farmer's plight, and greater authority to press the green gospel upon him.

The Hebrews in the Old Testament had all sorts of sacred places: sacred hills like Mount Hermon, sacred rivers like the Jordan, and of course the sacred burial fields. This did not imply that God was regarded as absent from the rest of the country; on the contrary, by making particular places holy, they were celebrating God's love for the whole natural order, for every mountain, every river and every field. Similarly, by treating the flora within our own burial fields and our own gardens as sacred, we are proclaiming the holiness of every field and every flower.

YEAST AND LIGHT – AND BELLS?

Older people in villages often say that when they went to church as children, it was always full. They recall that every pew from the front to the back was packed, and that they and the other children were forced to sit absolutely still and silent during the interminable sermon and prayers – quite unlike today's ill-disciplined youngsters! On hearing these recollections, the parson and the younger church-goers are liable to feel depressed and demoralised, wondering what has caused the congregation to drop to a mere handful in a single lifetime.

Closer questioning, however, reveals a quite different picture. Those who remember a full church six or seven decades ago are usually not regular church-goers themselves, nor were they as children. They attended worship only at the major festivals, especially Christmas, Easter and harvest, and in the confusion of old memories they imagine that the bustling congregations then were typical of every Sunday. A more accurate impression can be gained from old registers of services, where they can still be found. In most villages the numbers recorded for normal Sundays in 1920 or 1930 are only slightly greater than the figures today; and, since the clergy have always been inclined to err on the generous side, one may conclude the congregations have barely altered in size.

The fact is that the English have never been keen church-goers. Complaints about small congregations go back a thousand years, as do anxieties that the bulk of church-goers are elderly, so that the church will die with them. The only times the pews have been regularly full were in periods when church attendance was legally enforced, with severe fines for absences. Even in the Victorian heyday of the village church, most labourers spent Sunday morning in bed or in the pub, unless the squire or his wife dragooned them into Matins.

Karl Barth, the great German theologian, ascribed our religious indifference to 'the Englishmen's incurably Pelagian attitude to faith'. Pelagius, the only theologian from these shores to father a major heresy, taught that the individual is saved by good works, acting in a kind and generous fashion towards others, and avoiding dishonesty and cruelty. In his schema there is no place for divine grace, except as a source of moral courage. This, as Barth observed, gives little or no purpose to worship, since a person can behave well without ever uttering a prayer or singing a hymn. There is, sadly, much truth in Barth's strictures. A parson need only stroll along his village street to be bombarded with Pelagian remarks: 'I can be a good Christian without coming to church,' says one friendly parishioner; 'I always try to act in a Christian manner, but I don't have time to pray,' adds another; 'Christianity is all about being a good neighbour,' opines a third. Add to this our embarrassment at any outward expression of belief or emotion, then it is hardly surprising that most of our compatriots prefer to keep their religion strictly private.

Nevertheless, although they will not attend its services, most English people hold their church in great respect and affection. They want a parson in their midst who is devout in his prayers and blameless in his morality. They are reassured by the sound of the bells on Sunday morning, reminding them that the ancient rhythm of worship goes on (even if their only response is to draw the bedclothes tighter round their shoulders). They are comforted by the sight of the spire against the setting sun, as they take their dogs for an evening walk; and when the country faces a crisis, or is grappling with problems beyond the grasp of politicians, they desire and expect the church to speak out, offering guidance and hope.

The beleaguered clergyman and his tiny flock may be tempted to treat such ineffectual goodwill with contempt, yet it is precisely how Jesus expected his community to be regarded. Following the imagery of Isaiah, he spoke of his disciples as 'light', shining on a hilltop to show people the truth of God, and in an even more powerful metaphor he referred to them as 'yeast', raising the moral and spiritual awareness of society as a whole. Rather than bemoaning the small numbers at services, clergy and laity should be delighted that their neighbours look to them for light and want them to be yeast, and should set about fulfilling these expectations with renewed vigour.

Seen in this way, the Pelagian heresy ceases to be a stumbling-block against faith, but becomes the first step towards it. In speaking of Christianity as a moral system, people are expressing their desire for Christians to embody that morality, and so provide a standard to which others can aspire. In family matters Christians are expected to enjoy loving and stable marriages, and to exert a gentle yet firm and consistent discipline on their children. Within the village Christians are looked on to lead the way in helping those in need, and in contributing time and money to local projects, while in the wider world of work and business they are supposed to be scrupulously honest and fair. When a parson or leading lay person is divorced, or acts selfishly and deceitfully, the outcry and derision stem not merely from delight at seeing high-minded people fall, but also from profound shock that a moral light has been snuffed out. On the other hand, when Christians prove faithful, loving and generous, they serve as an inspiration to those around them. This in turn may prompt a few to ask the source of their moral strength, and they will be told that it is not individual will-power, but the grace of Christ.

As red-eyed bishops often complain, emerging from another lengthy and fruitless conference among themselves, it is extraordinarily difficult for the church to speak with one voice on public issues. There are Christians at every point of the political spectrum, able to quote verses from Scripture in support of their ideals, yet when the church manages to articulate a common national interest, and expresses the solidarity of all classes and races, it can have an astonishing impact. Thus the *Faith in the City* report is remembered not for its detailed proposals, but for the moral passion it brought to bear on the scandal of urban squalor; in this way it became the focus for the whole country's concern. Equally, in a single village it is not for the local church to air its view on the merits of new street lights, or whether exotic ducks should be purchased for the village pond. But when in the parish magazine the parson, backed by his laity, urges people to treat a band of gypsies parked outside the village with charity, or berates the parish for allowing some of its senior residents to shiver for want of fuel during a cold winter, his words carry the sting of a hard slap. While some may complain, others will take water out to the gypsies, and offer to fetch wood for an elderly neighbour, and all in their own way will respect the church for standing up for its beliefs.

In the ancient stories of saints which fed our childhood consciences, we admired most those self-effacing men and women who performed secret acts of charity, such as Nicholas dropping gold coins down a chimney as dowries for three impoverished girls. So too as adults we know that our own small acts of charity should be as covert as the deeds allow: in the moral economy of God the force of our charity grows in proportion to our own modesty and reticence. When the Christians in a village go about quietly visiting the sick, taking people to appointments at hospital, offering a friendly ear to those in distress (and asking for neither gratitude nor reward), their loving spirit spreads unseen through the community. People throughout the village feel warmer towards those around them, and more willing to do a good turn themselves. In short, those local saints act as agents raising the morale of the entire parish, like yeast in dough.

Once we can see ourselves as light and yeast, our anxiety about numbers in pews dissolves. Being frail and insecure human beings, we cannot help wanting some outward affirmation of our efforts, and the quantity of people coming to hear our sermons and share our worship is the obvious yardstick. Yet in most villages God forces humility and trust upon us: we must humbly accept that our spiritual ministry will be recognised only by a small group; and at the same time we must trust that God is using that ministry for a larger purpose. Our task within the community is simply to be faithful disciples of Jesus, acting as he directs. God, in his good time and mysterious way, will use our faithfulness to soften the hearts of those around us, and thence, according to his will, enable some to receive the gift of faith. Thus, so long as we have remained true to our Master, it is God's business how many come to services. Indeed, even in the first Christian church in Jerusalem, described in the Acts of the Apostles, the members' sole achievement was to 'win the goodwill of the people'; it was God who 'added to their numbers day by day'.

If yeast and light are apt images of Christian mission drawn from the Bible, an equally good image can be found within our church towers. The Christians within a village are like the bells which ring out over its rooftops on Sunday morning. There are not many of them, yet everyone in the village is aware of them. They are gentle and reassuring, yet at times they disturb people. They have been there a very long time, yet they never go out of date. People are slow to respond to their call, but they are regarded with great love and goodwill. To everyone they are a sign of hope and a source of comfort. Incidentally, the metaphor of bells is peculiarly rural and English. All but a handful of our four thousand peals of bells are in the countryside, and in England, alone among Christian countries, the bells are tuned to play in harmony with one another and are rung in musical sequence. That, of course, completes the metaphor: the Christians in a village need only live in harmony with one another and with their neighbours, and God will play the sweetest and most powerful music upon them, for all to hear.